DEEDA BLAIR: FOOD, FLOWERS & FANTASY

Deeda Blair in her apartment on the East River in Manhattan, wearing a navy dress by Ralph Rucci, 2013. Photo by Julia Hetta for *T Magazine,* the *New York Times*.

DEEDA BLAIR: FOOD, FLOWERS & FANTASY

Edited by Deborah Needleman

RIZZOLI NEW YORK

New York · Paris · London · Milan

INTRODUCTION

9   On Deeda
        Andrew Solomon

PART I
THOUGHTS & REFLECTIONS

29   On Entertaining
45   On Inspiration

PART II
FANTASY MENUS

78   Lunch at Haga Pavilion
92   Sunday Lunch at La Fiorentina
106   Picnic on a Visit to Egyptian Treasures
118   Luncheon at Château du Jonchet
134   Dinner at Pavlovsk Palace
146   Dinner at the Petit Trianon

PART III
RECIPES

162   Soups
168   First Courses
176   Lunches & Salads
186   Pasta
192   Poultry & Meat
202   Fish & Lobster
208   Vegetables
214   Cakes, Tarts, Soufflés & Cookies
226   Ice Cream, Sorbets & Fruit Desserts
234   Sauces & Special Favorites

RESOURCES

243   Favorite Sources
246   Recipe Index
249   Photo Credits
250   The Deeda Blair Research Initiative
252   Acknowledgments

The Blairs' living room in Washington, D.C., 2001. Deeda has the same tableau in the front hall of her current apartment in Manhattan. Photo by Eric Boman for *House Beautiful*.

To the loves of my life,
William McCormick Blair Jr.
and
William McCormick Blair III

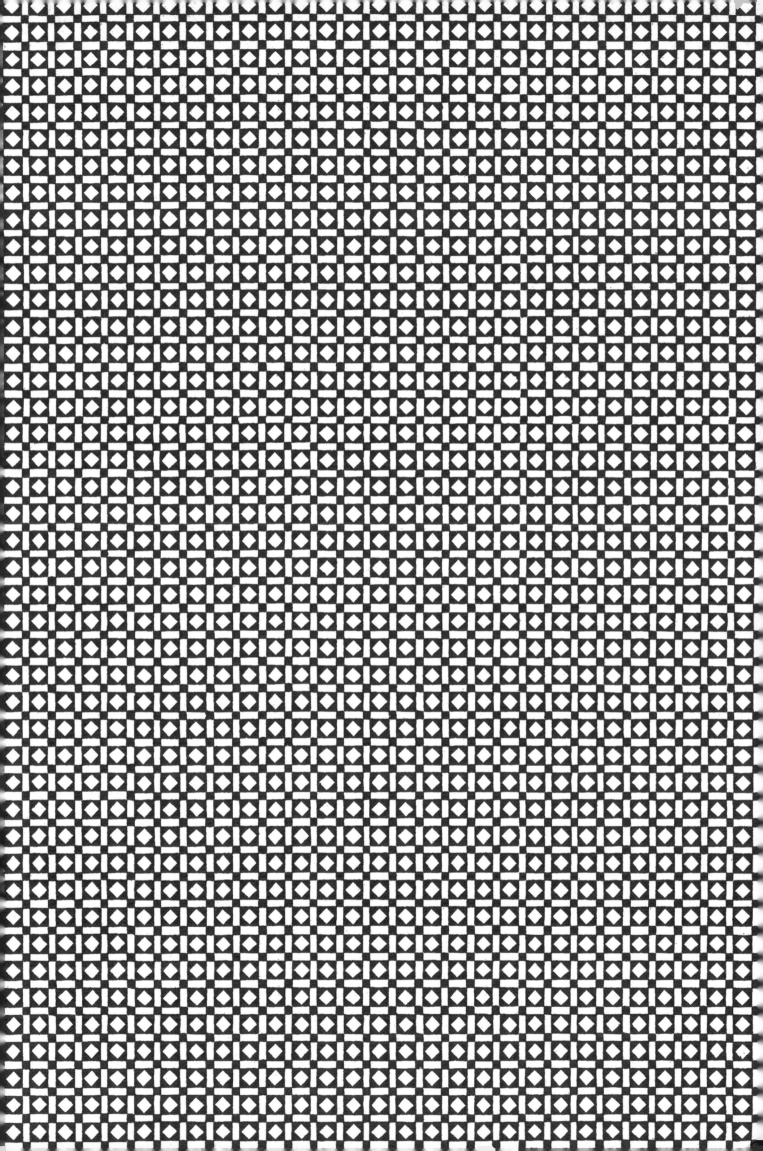

ON DEEDA

Andrew Solomon

Deeda shortly after her wedding to William McCormick Blair Jr.,
wearing a dress by Givenchy, 1961. Photo by Helmut Newton for *Vogue*.

T he word "elegant" is in regular use in both fashion and science; it can describe a certain understated self-assurance manifest in a choice of clothing, an arrangement of furniture, or the setting of a table—and, equally, the underlying structures of the universe or the routine transcription of RNA. It perfectly describes Deeda Blair. Most style mavens are surprised by her scientific expertise, and scientists are astonished by her style. If one penetrates those disparate worlds, however, one soon finds that neurobiologists credit her deep interest in helping them think through difficult questions, and that fashionistas must employ metaphors from eighteenth-century France to describe the impeccable way she dresses and entertains.

Deeda's couture is severe and simple, the kind that only the knowing eye can identify as couture. Her trademark bouffant has not changed in sixty years, but it does not feel dated; it feels Deeda. Her apartment, all pale gray, is like being inside a pearl; it is a study in discipline. She entertains in a way that is both up-to-date and timeless; the dishes she serves could have appeared in a Capri picnic in 1950, at a court supper in Versailles under the Sun King, or in a smug New York cafe that opened last Tuesday. The place settings are likewise neither old nor new: or perhaps they are both old and new. Something exquisitely painted for a French collector sits surprisingly easily atop a plain white charger, and the napkins: Well, who ever thought so much pleasure could be located in the precision of folded linen? Pretension lies in striving to be who you are not; Deeda tries, rather, to be even more of who she is. And who she is outstrips what she says or does; her gentle way of insisting on people's best selves enables their accomplishments.

Deeda mixes austerity with intimacy, and at my first dinner with her, I found her both aloof and engaging; she seemed to offer only an impression of herself, but to see the rest of us more boldly than we'd intended. Several accomplished scientists were in the klatch that evening, and Deeda asked questions with her characteristic quiet intensity, as though conducting discreet but critical interviews on behalf of the Nobel committee. Her style is at once embracing and exclusive, as though it didn't bother with most of the world but bothered with *you*, whoever you might be on that particular evening.

Ruffles can disguise a multitude of sins, but Deeda's clothes are distinguished for their underlying architecture, and the way she sports them reflects her understanding of their construction. She's one of the only people I know who can wear a jacket with insight. "Some of Deeda's signature pieces might at first be mistaken for clerical garb, but then an open seam reveals a flash of chiffon-veiled skin, or a silk tulle petticoat reveals a surface animated by ostrich filaments or gilt metal sequins," Harold Koda, the former head of the Costume Institute at the Metropolitan Museum of Art, explained. Her monochrome palette in both her dress and her apartment's decoration underscores the luxury without conjuring opulence. "What I love about being seated next to her at a dinner," he told me, "is the conspiratorial breathiness of her conversation. You have to lean in to hear her describe the black steel sparkle of a Tula table she coveted in Pavlovsk, or some evolving protocol in oncology, or her preference for the spare draping of eighteenth-century curtains, or the diagnostic tools for bipolar disorder. She would be accused of being a sybarite if it weren't for the conceptual rigor she applies to her aesthetics." Deeda describes her own mind as "zigzag"; she darts from topic to topic as if conversation were a bravado act on a high wire. It's thrilling to follow her free associations from topic to topic.

Once, Deeda gave me a beautiful notebook. She has always liked small geometrics, and such a pattern made the cover of a collection of her recipes, a gift that has inspired this volume. Some of these recipes are so precise and require such care that I knew they would be beyond my ken, but others are surprisingly simple, fresh ways to address familiar ingredients. It's my favorite book for entertaining because the instructions are sufficient to get it right; each dish suits a different occasion and also a different mood. Sometimes, I like to imagine going full Deeda: having almost everything match and then a few things cleverly not match, achieving a restrained asymmetry as much Japanese as Western. Her way of setting the table is a recherché gesture to indicate that while the courts of Europe are rather magnificent, America can do something new with all this. Deeda's entertaining is intensely personal and self-invented, but also informed by history—rather the way the Renaissance was informed by fifth-century Athens. Deeda's apartment has the luxurious drape of fashion, a Balenciaga extravagance. She always has the details on couture pieces redone to suit her—sometimes multiple times over an ensemble's lifetime. And she is always questioning the scientists whose work she supports. She customizes the world.

Deeda was hardly brought up to be an activist. She grew up in Chicago, went to the Convent of the Sacred Heart for Girls to be educated, and made her debut in 1949. She attended a two-year junior college and lived a vigorously social life, traveling widely. Soon after her first marriage ended, she met her true love, William McCormick Blair Jr., at Eunice and Sargent Shriver's house. Bill was a partner at a law firm with Adlai Stevenson at the time and was a Kennedy intimate; Eunice was the chaperone through their courtship. Shortly after Bill

Deeda by Juergen Teller for *W*, Paris, 1999.

was appointed Kennedy's ambassador to Denmark, Deeda married him at Frederiksborg Castle. Bill was later Johnson's ambassador to the Philippines. During these postings, both Bill and Deeda proved that diplomacy is achieved not only through the intense negotiation through which most diplomats pursue their goals, but also through grace.

Bill had introduced his socially literate wife to the medical philanthropist Mary Lasker, who helped build up the National Institutes of Health (NIH) and led the War on Cancer. Deeda told me that at Sacred Heart, she had worn "the world's ugliest uniform" and had not been allowed to study biology, and she reacted against the first problem with fashion and against the second with Mary Lasker. She and Lasker were soon best of friends, summering together in the South of France at La Fiorentina. Lasker had a gift for leading people with power to those who could conceptualize medical quandaries; she would have Greta Garbo and Princess Grace to dinner with Michael DeBakey (the distinguished heart surgeon) or James Watson (the co-discoverer of the structure of DNA). Lasker saw that Deeda could carry that tradition forward. In 1965, Deeda became vice president of the Albert and Mary Lasker Foundation. Today, she is vice president emeritus.

While living a glamorous life entertaining at home, decorating a splendid house with Billy Baldwin, and going to couture shows twice a year, Deeda was also now receiving a neo-academic education, her mind fully engaged with abstruse science. She operated with an urgent deliberateness that echoed her personal style. Lasker was on the National Cancer Advisory Board, so Deeda focused initially on cancer research. She met the scientists, asked them questions, read their papers. When she visited New York, she would stay with Lasker, who would introduce her to more physicians. "Mary asked a great friend, David Karnofsky, at Memorial Sloan-Kettering, to take me on," Deeda recalled. "And that was the most extraordinary learning experience—whether it was rounds, whether it was lectures, whether he was showing me how to dissect chicken embryos and look for liver damage. He made me feel that there was a role for a layperson." Soon enough, Deeda was on the Breast Cancer Task Force treatment committee at NIH, where she was the only woman. She also served for twelve years on the board of the American Cancer Society, where she joined the research committee. She began going to jury meetings for the Lasker Awards, the most prestigious medical prizes in the United States. She was a voracious learner.

Soon oncologists were talking about the sudden uptick in a previously exotic cancer called Kaposi's sarcoma, occurring mostly among gay men. Deeda was

Previous spread: Deeda's living-room walls in New York finished in pale blue-gray Venetian plaster, the floors are covered in white deck paint with a rug of gray and white cotton. She replaced the moldings with pilasters topped with Corinthian capitals.
Photo by Julia Hetta for *T Magazine*, the *New York Times*.

Deeda with scientists from around the world at the International AIDS Conference in Paris, mid-1980s.

Deeda's first public speech, mid-1980s, where she received a leadership award with funds for the Harvard AIDS Institute and the Georgetown Lombardi Cancer Center.

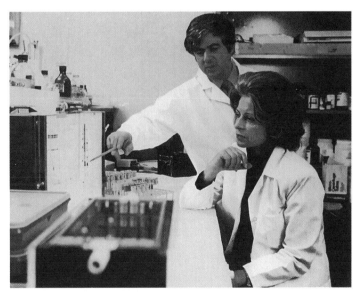

Deeda with Dr. Max Essex in his lab at the Harvard School of Public Health, late 1980s.

Deeda with her son, William, in Manila, Philippines, 1965.

there for the initial meetings on the subject, which led her to be in the front lines of emerging AIDS research at a time when the disease and its victims were shunned. Deeda approached the illness with compassion but without sentimentality in her usual quiet, behind-the-scenes, shockingly effective way.

She joined the visiting committee at the Harvard School of Public Health and worked with the HIV team there, which was led by Max Essex. "AIDS was the first time I ever really asked anyone for money," Deeda said. "We needed to know how it was transmitted, and Max wanted to study that. And I asked Mary Lasker for $50,000. A couple of years later, I identified another foundation whose progenitors had been extraordinarily generous. I invited them for lunch and was so embarrassed that tears were going down my cheeks. I said, 'You have already given us so much, but we've got to have a laser cell sorter.' And then I rattled off what a laser cell sorter was. And they said, 'Deeda, stop. We will do everything in our power to get you your laser cell sorter.' And they did it within three weeks."

Deeda established a trademark style. Who but Deeda would introduce Nobel laureates to Hubert de Givenchy, or come home, a few months later, from the Paris couture shows with $267,000 for an automatic sequencer to identify African variants of HIV? Essex once wrote that Deeda always had "an understanding of the whole interlocking process of getting things done . . . and sees one thing always—hope." When Dr. Michael Gottesman at the NIH once said, "Deeda Blair has incredible taste," he was speaking not of her stylish entertaining, but of her "incredible taste in identifying creative science." Deeda has since served on the boards of the Harvard AIDS Institute, the Scripps Research Institute and numerous other research organizations. When I asked her how she seduced so many people into supporting the causes she cares about, she told me her secret: "enthusiasm."

She was married to Bill for fifty-four years, until his death in 2015 at the age of 98. He took pleasure in indulging her, and his support was the engine of her transformation into a woman whose style was matched by substance. "I had the world's most heavenly husband," she said. "He just got me; he just got it. And he always gave me tremendous independence to pursue my interests. Independence with applause."

With that independence, in the early 1980s, Deeda began translating all the knowledge she had gleaned during her nonprofit years into a career. She would set up researchers who were inventing new compounds with venture capitalists. In 1987, she became a consultant to Sandoz pharmaceuticals. The cancer researcher Dr. Gregory Curt has said, "Biologically I think of her as an enzyme, a protein that causes reactions that would not happen without it." She began grappling with new subjects, ever more difficult ones.

In 2004, tragedy struck when Deeda and Bill lost their only child, who had bipolar disorder, to suicide at age 41. "The manic periods were so difficult for everyone, and for him, I think, also," she said. "And the depressed periods he concealed. He would come over and curl up on the sofa in the downstairs rooms and just sleep. He was very unreachable. And you felt so frustrated, but you didn't know how to do anything." Later, she added, "The thing that haunts you forever is that you can't understand what is going on in the mind of someone you care about. That phrase, 'the impenetrable internal world.' You live with the thought he did not feel his life was valuable. You feel guilt that he experienced a lack of alignment with what he perceived as our hopes and expectations. We all have moments of feeling overwhelmed but to look back now and know that he felt that way almost constantly. One will always wonder if something could have been done differently. He hated being sick, loathed intrusive questioning and medications."

After his death, she became increasingly interested in the brain. "Going back to work was very important," she said at the time. "I went to a meeting at the National Institutes of Health and saw that I could stay all day and function. It's a terrific distraction."

She and Bill relocated to New York following the death of their son, doing up their apartment at River House, which is featured in the images throughout this book. In New York, Deeda was a co-founder of the Alexandria Summit—a series of conferences at which leading science researchers gather to exchange ideas. I've attended and participated in these summits, and they are the best science going. Working there with Lynne Zydowsky and Joel Marcus, Deeda helped curate the gatherings, which included a mix of academic and clinical research scientists; pharmaceutical and biotech companies; representatives from the government and advocacy groups; venture capital firms; and nonprofit foundations.

Her seriousness can be almost unsettling; it seems to come from a strict moral center. But if she holds others to high standards, she always meets them herself. In her vision statement for one of the summits, Deeda wrote, "How do we do science better? Unprecedented collaborations for cancer drug development must now be created, leading the way to rationally designed combination therapies targeted to molecular pathways to accelerate predictive, individualized treatment. Going forward, doors need to be opened widely and risks taken."

Deeda with her husband, Bill Blair, in Venice, Italy, 1991. Photo by Ellen Graham.

ON DEEDA

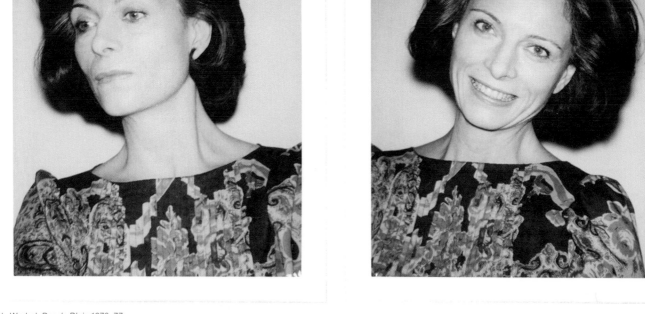

Andy Warhol, *Deeda Blair*, 1976–77.
Polacolor Type 108. 4 ¼ x 3 ⅜ inches. (10.8 x 8.6 cm).
© 2022 The Andy Warhol Foundation for the Visual Arts, Inc. /
Licensed by Artists Rights Society (ARS), New York.

ON DEEDA

Deeda and William coming up from the woods at the house in Washington, D.C., 1972.
Photo by Horst P. Horst.

In honor of her son, she started the Deeda Blair Research Initiative for Disorders of the Brain at the Foundation for the National Institute of Health, through which she sponsors cutting edge research. "Everyone wants to fund projects that they know will succeed," she said. "I want to fund young researchers I believe in, the ones whose work is still too preliminary for most major grants, the ones who are deploying their imagination in fresh and surprising ways." She originally assumed that the program would kick in after she died, but friends persuaded her to oversee its inception, so she assembled a board of accomplished brain research scholars and began to choose projects that might engender a better world.

It is only when you have come to know Deeda rather well that you can see that her fashion and science are not in opposition, that her glamorous side and her rigorous side fit together neatly. She doesn't buy all new clothes every season; she intuits what will look good for decades, buys sparingly, and wears them accordingly. In her apartment, she pairs a delicious sofa designed for her by Billy Baldwin with Louis XVI chairs and a Jansen table. There, she entertains; her table is smaller than it was in Copenhagen, but then Deeda is all about intimate conversation, and if you come to dinner at her house, you will be talking with her—though she can hold back when she sees her guests fully engaging one another. "Real elegance is having convictions," Deeda said to me. She has them in all areas of her life.

Deeda's trademark irony is that she is a cancer expert who never stops smoking. There are few images of Deeda that don't show a sinuous line of smoke trailing up from her lips and blending in with the calligraphy of her gray-streaked hair. "I began when I was 14, for defiance and rebellion. And I really enjoy it. As I'm advancing on antiquity, I'm part of a spiral CT study, and they give you this form, 'Are you going to consider giving it up?' 'Would you like us to prescribe a patch?' I always seem to shock them when I say, 'Well, maybe next time.'"

She once told me that she studies as if she were going to live forever and lives as if she were going to die tomorrow. She quests after abstruse knowledge she is not yet qualified to absorb, then ratchets up her qualifications with the energy of the present moment. "What I've liked a lot about my life is being catalytic, putting people together that will work well. It sounds sort of bossy, but it just sometimes clicks. Will I leave a scratch on a rock? No. There are so many people who do magnificent, significant things, and I don't. But what difference does it make whether you're remembered fifty years from now? It's this life that you're leading." My internist said, 'Deeda, you've got to cut down.

Why do you work so hard?' I don't like to answer 'why' questions. Maybe what, but not why. But I mumbled, 'Well, I'd sort of like to achieve something.'"

The combination of chic and intellect can be forbidding. But Deeda is also a supremely kind person. She has read everything I've written in the last decades, often before it was published, and she has never disappointed in either insight or generosity. The key to living like Deeda is choosing the right friends and then being interested in them and then hearing them with compassion. There is no better listener. I have never felt impatient at Deeda's table, and I have always known that I could call her in a moment of need—or, indeed, a moment of simple boredom. She exalts the moment; you cannot but feel chosen when she gives you her focus, which is always inflected with a wry sense of humor and that trademark elegance. The way she is as a friend and the way she is throwing a luncheon are one and the same.

This book is an instruction manual for enduring style. I will consult it frequently as I figure out my own parties, but I think my grandchildren, should they eventually come along, are likely to do the same. When I am feeling stuck and I know that the table looks wrong, or the food isn't up to par, or the seating isn't working, I think, "What would Deeda do?" Because she is among my dearest friends, I am lucky enough to guess well, which gives me an advantage. Now that advantage is available to everyone who has this book in hand. If you aren't sure how to make your party work, you need look no further than these pages. Go full Deeda: be curious, combine intellectual and corporeal style, stick to regal bearing, put people at ease without ever giving yourself away, read everything, know what you don't know, rely equally on intuition and research, set a splendid table and populate it with brilliant friends—it's a technique that never misses.

ON ENTERTAINING

The Blairs entering Katharine Graham's seventieth birthday party in Washington, D.C., 1987.
Photo by Guy DeLort.

It is in many ways out of character for me to write a book, as privacy is very important to me. My desire to do so is twofold. One reason is that I would hate to see the recipes collected here—enjoyed and perfected over so many years—vanish. The other is to raise money for my foundation, the Deeda Blair Research Initiative for Disorders of the Brain (see page 250).

Many of the recipes in this book date back to my past. A few come from my grandmother and mother; others are dishes I've been served by generous friends in their homes or on my travels. Some I've taken from famous cooks or cookbooks, and still others come from trying to crack the mystery and replicate dishes from favorite restaurants. Nearly all have been adapted by me—altered in their proportions or ingredients or amended in other substantial ways.

I began collecting recipes long ago, keeping them together in files. Over time, the files gave way to a three-ring binder, and eventually, when recipe requests from friends became frequent, we stored the recipes on the computer to share them more easily. For very close friends, I would often make a copy of the original three-ring binder, cover it in patterned Italian paper that I collected for years in Venice, and illustrate the inside with photographs of inspiring paintings, along with handwritten notes and a few drawings by me on some of the recipes showing how I like to assemble or serve the dishes. Those gifts, given at Christmastime, are in many ways the model for this book.

What really has never varied for me, despite the many changes and trends in cooking, is the food I like and how I like to serve it. If a recipe was successful and delicious at the time, it remains so to me. Many things that delight me, such as molds and aspics, are quite out of fashion, and it is partly for that reason that they continue to surprise and delight my guests. And while many of these dishes are rich, the portions never are. I dislike looking at a plate filled high with food.

When entertaining at home, I always serve three courses. The first is usually not large—a soup, pasta, or salad. That just feels right. Then for a second course, a somewhat larger serving of the main dish that leaves room for dessert. I love desserts; I often start planning the menu with dessert in mind. I then choose the other courses with a consideration of the time of year and what is in season. It is my hope that these recipes are timeless. They are somewhat different from most home cooking today, and served in moderate, healthy portions.

As this is a book about cooking for others, I must explain something about the way I entertain now, which comes not only from a lifetime of attending events and dinners, but from giving more than my share of them. Except on rare occasions, every meal I serve now is an intimate affair with two to four or, at most, six guests at the table. I find small gatherings where people can have a relaxed easy evening more pleasurable and interesting than a large party. You are also able to offer better food to four guests than to twenty-four. For this reason, this book includes no suggestions for large events, cocktail parties, or buffets; however, the recipes can always be doubled or multiplied further, if desired.

When my husband, Bill, and I moved to New York in 2004, I did not even consider a typical dining room in our apartment. In my living room, I have a fifty-inch round table set in front of a window overlooking the East River with four French armchairs around it, and an additional two chairs against the wall, in case they are needed. In the library there is an oval black table, frequently with a maidenhair fern on it, for quick lunches. Even in Washington, D.C., where we lived before New York, our dining room did not resemble a dining room. The table was surrounded by two big laurel trees in huge Chinese jardinieres, and it looked out onto the garden's miniature Kingsville boxwood hedges. Billy Baldwin created ravishing pale lettuce-green curtains that made the room feel connected to the outdoors. Near the table, there was a niche originally meant to hold a sideboard that we filled with book shelves and antique porcelain flowers. Two eighteenth-century botanical books were always upright and open, displaying their illustrations, and I'd change the pages from time to time to feature different plants. Our life, however, was different then. We did have to entertain in larger and more elaborate ways, and so I could, when necessary, add two more round tables in that room to seat twenty-four people.

Many years were spent entertaining frequently and on a larger scale when Bill was ambassador to Denmark and the Philippines, and later, when he was the first general director of the Kennedy Center for the Performing Arts in Washington, D.C. When we were living in Copenhagen, for my birthday in December each year, Bill would get a copy of the latest James Bond movie before it was released. We'd rent a screening room and invite friends, ambassadors, embassy colleagues, and dancers from the Royal Danish Ballet, and then have a supper at the residence after the screening. Bill had an uncanny ability to arrange seating plans (he could do six or sixty skillfully in one pass). This tradition continued after we moved to Manila, as Bill was again able to get many of the new American movies before they were released. These movie nights became a fairly regular event.

Opposite: A side table set for lunch in Deeda's living room in New York. On the easel is an eighteenth-century watercolor by Hubert Robert. Photo by Ngoc Minh Ngo.

The Blairs at home in Washington, D.C., 1972. Photo by Horst P. Horst for *Vogue*.

The Blairs' Washington dining room designed by Billy Baldwin, 1972. Photo by Horst P. Horst for *Vogue*.

Following spread: Deeda's dining table set for dinner with a tablecloth by Mitchell Denburg, plates by Tiffany & Co., and a lilac sculpture by Carmen Almon. Photo by Ngoc Minh Ngo.

ON ENTERTAINING

The Blairs' fiftieth wedding anniversary celebration, La Grenouille, 2011.

Deeda likes to repot nursery plants, like this white rose, into pretty containers for the house.

Lilacs and white roses from the garden with ceramic vegetables.

A generous arrangement of ranunculus, a favorite flower of Deeda's.

A bouquet for the bedroom.

Bill's seventy-fifth birthday party, 1991, with Carroll Petrie, Bill, Lauren Bacall (laughing), Dr. Étienne-Émile Baulieu, Nan Kempner.

Table setting and flowers by Deeda at home in Washington, D.C., 1991. Photo by Quentin Bacon.

Roses cut from the garden.

A birthday dinner at La Grenouille, early 1990s, with Jackie Onassis, Khalil Rizk, Deeda.

ON ENTERTAINING

When we arrived in Washington, the Kennedy Center was little more than a very large hole in the ground, and we were constantly giving fundraising dinners and luncheons at home to raise money for its construction, decoration, and, eventually, to celebrate its opening. Dinners were given all over Washington, and for ours we had to put the almost eighty people who attended in our basement, because our dining room was too small. The playroom and office furniture were banished. I hung fabric over the brick walls, and the plates were kept warm in the sauna! We did a spring gala before the fall opening, and after it opened, we gave three more large dinners: one to inaugurate the opera house (where Leonard Bernstein's *MASS* was performed); one for the symphony hall; and another for the theater.

For these events, we did not use caterers, but rather our own family cook—supplemented by helpers—working from my recipes. I have been fortunate to have wonderful cooks at home over the years with whom I worked very closely in the kitchen—training them, guiding them, and updating the recipes accord-ing to new thinking. These recipes do not require a high level of skill or talent. I have made all of them for myself over the years, and often for guests when the cook was unavailable. Bill always felt strongly that we should never experiment on guests—good advice, I believe—so we would always do at least two trials of new recipes. One aspect of my life that was quite different from most was that I had a husband who always came home for lunch, so I tried out new dishes on him all the time.

On a more personal note, I also gave many dinners with Mary Lasker, the great science philanthropist, to help support scientific research. Most of these were done in an effort to increase the budget for the National Institutes of Health (NIH). The guest lists were very targeted, and someone once commented, "My god, the whole Congressional Appropriations Committee is here!" But Mary and I always mixed important decision makers, members of congress, and senators with leading scientists, interesting friends, and journalists. Memorable among these fundraising dinners were several very large ones for the first International AIDS Conference in Washington in 1987, and two for the Foundation for the National Institutes of Health, with 400 guests each, held at the Library of Congress.

Perhaps you can see why, after so many years of large entertainments, when Bill and I were free to do things just the way we wanted, we chose mostly to give small intimate dinners where people could have in-depth conversations. It is not that I never give large parties, but the few we've given since moving

Opposite: The dining table in the living room with quince branches by sculptor Vladimir Kanevsky. Photo by Ngoc Minh Ngo.

ON ENTERTAINING

to New York, such as a birthday party for Jayne Wrightsman and a celebration of our own fiftieth wedding anniversary, we have held at favorite restaurants, most commonly in the room upstairs at La Grenouille, rather than at home. The former owner of La Grenouille, Charles Masson, would graciously allow me to use a few of my own recipes for these parties, along with my favorites of his, some of which are included here. At every gathering, I made sure there were glorious flowers on the table. I like to keep things simple, but original, and surprising.

ON INSPIRATION

Sightseeing along the Dalmatian coast, 1960s. Snapshot by Cecil Beaton, a guest on the trip.

My life has admittedly been one of privilege. I think I have had my share
of sadness and grief, but so, too, have I had great freedom and opportu-
nity, having traveled widely, and seen and read much. On the question
of whether one is born with taste or whether it is acquired, my view is strongly
that one is not born with it. It is the result of careful consideration and observation. It is partly a question of exposure, of seeing beautiful things, but more
important are the qualities of openness and curiosity. Taste, I believe, comes from
being open to the influence of other people and of art, books, travel, gardens,
rooms, and houses.

Several people have had enormous influence on my life, inspiring its direction
and the development of my interests, intellect, and aesthetic. Many whom I
write about here and in the next chapter were passionate collectors. Collecting is
not buying just to have things; rather, it is a form of education and appreciation.
The things in a collection should be good examples of their kind. I have collected
a few French eighteenth-century chairs, a bit of porcelain, ceramics, and a lot of
books. I have very little art on the walls of my apartment, and none on the walls
of the living room. People provide so much color to a room, and I prefer to talk to
them in an atmosphere of serenity. But another reason is that I can't afford what
I would actually want to look at every day. This does not make me sad in any way.
I love the light coming in from the East River and how it plays on the Venetian-
plaster pale blue walls, as well the empty space in the room and the ferns and
flowers and things that I have on the tables and the mantel. I have one quite good
Hubert Robert drawing done in the eighteenth century in my living room, but
it is set upon an easel rather than on the wall. Looking at it gives me so much
pleasure. In the library—a room that is more layered in its decoration—I have a
serene and lovely large painting by Kenzo Okada on the wall, and propped on
the bookshelves are a few framed botanical watercolors that came with me from
Washington, as well as a huge number of books. One should be appreciative
of wondrous things, but should also understand one's own situation, and live
according to one's preferences and passions.

The following brief chronology of my life, organized around descriptions of
the people who have most inspired me, offers, I think, some explanation of how
I found my own taste.

My Early Years

Our lives are often a reaction to our experiences, whether for good or bad. We are formed in many ways by our childhoods—and often, as in my case, by a decision to define myself differently from my upbringing. My mother was a devout Catholic who was very worried that I was not as devoted as she. At the Convent of the Sacred Heart in Chicago, where I went for twelve years of schooling, I was constantly breaking the rules. It seemed I was always being kept late to copy out scripture on lined paper, which did, I'll admit, result in decent penmanship.

My love of fashion and the desire to customize my clothing and my surroundings were a response to spending twelve years in the most hideous shapeless blue school uniforms. When I was allowed to dress up for the fortnightly club dances, my mother insisted on picking out my evening dresses—stiff ruffly things in pinks or yellows, which I hated. I longed for black or white. For college, I was not allowed to apply to Vassar, where I wanted to go, but was sent to Bennett Junior College. Not surprisingly, I hated weekends there and all the beer drinking. I preferred to go into New York and visit museums and the theater. One time in New York, I bought a great black dress. After that, on most New York weekends, I would go to the theater without a ticket, frequently alone, in my one black dress. I looked quite okay, and most nights I'd get a great seat that the box office might have been saving for performers. I ended up sitting next to fascinating people like Gregory Peck and Laurence Olivier. After Bennett, I attended a New York fashion school called Tobé-Coburn, which had a course on Paris and French couture, which I found interesting, in large part because it included a map of all the Parisian ateliers.

I very much wanted a different kind of life from the one I had in Chicago, and it became my dream to visit Paris. While my parents traveled widely, the inspiration for how I could set my own path came largely through friends—many of them determined, intelligent, imaginative, and hard-working women—and my adventures with them.

Eunice Shriver
A Dedication to Others

The first really strong, influential friendship I had was with Eunice Shriver, John F. Kennedy's sister, who lived next door to my parents in Chicago. Eunice was older than I was, but we became very close and enduring friends, and did so much together, including horseback riding, kite flying, and playing tennis. I loved her children—Bobby was around two when Eunice and I became friends. I was there when Maria was born, and Timmy is my godchild. I met my future husband at a dinner party at Eunice's. During the meal, I kept glancing down the table at a good-looking man with dark, brooding eyes who turned out to be one William Blair. He and Eunice were very close friends, but perhaps because he was almost two decades older than I was and a lifelong bachelor, she hadn't thought to put us together. At that time, Bill was a lawyer in Chicago and a key political advisor to Adlai Stevenson, and I had recently moved home to Chicago after a difficult first marriage. We started seeing each other, and whenever both of us were in town, we would meet.

When Eunice took over the work of her family foundation, she steered its mission toward studying the causes of intellectual disabilities and finding ways to champion the lives of developmentally challenged children. I saw how diligently she worked and how dedicated she was to research and to learning all she could. I began to help her, and together we would seek out experts to share their knowledge with us. Eunice would ask the most provocative and interesting questions, and in response, we would receive a mini-seminar. Gradually, she realized the vital importance of athletics and physical activity on the well-being and self-esteem of children, especially those with mental disabilities, and

Adonis Brown, smiling, as Eunice Kennedy Shriver awards him with a gold medal at the International Special Olympics, Los Angeles, 1972.

she created the Special Olympics. In the beginning, she hosted summer camps on the property of her own house outside Washington, D.C. I watched as she became increasingly creative about her work for the foundation and about fundraising. Eventually, the Special Olympics outgrew her backyard, and its programs moved into large stadiums around the world with movie stars and singers added as spokespeople. It developed into an extraordinary and important international enterprise, positively affecting the lives of millions of children. Eunice also helped create the National Institute of Child Health and Human Development at NIH, which Congress later renamed in her honor.

When Eunice died, more than one hundred children who had participated in the Special Olympics came to her funeral and walked behind her casket. At the burial site, many put their gold medals in her grave. Eunice dedicated her life to helping others, and when you see someone work that hard and accomplish so much, you can't help but be impressed and inspired.

Hubert de Givenchy
The Lure of Paris

While living at home again, my parents invited me to join them on two of their round-the-world trips. The first included stops in Paris, Rome, Venice, and a tour of several Greek islands; the second, England, Egypt, India, Burma, Thailand, and Japan. At the time, I was obsessed with the clothes that Hubert de Givenchy had done for Audrey Hepburn in the movies *Sabrina* and *Funny Face*. So, before the first trip began, I went ahead of them to Paris to visit Givenchy. When I first arrived at his large atelier, Hubert was on the floor surrounded by dozens of fabric swatches, and he was sketching to the soundtrack from *Funny Face*. Hubert was somewhat shy, and his English was hesitant, and for my part, despite twelve years of classes at a convent school, my French was clumsy and halting. Yet, we managed to communicate. I ordered a suit, and then went off to have my hair cut by Alexandre.

At this time, Hubert was just beginning to create his own couture collections. He had been mentored by Cristóbal Balenciaga, whose clothes I revered, so I also made an appointment with the *directrice* at Balenciaga, Mademoiselle Renée. She was very nice to me and let me try on dozens of things for the sheer pleasure of it. She gave me a special price for *jeunes filles*, and

I bought a short evening coat in the heaviest cotton pique that was absolutely divine, which I wore to the theater and to dinners for years and years. From then on, until Balenciaga retired, I bought clothes there and at Givenchy. Later, Balenciaga made my wedding dress in a pale blue—on the advice of Diana Vreeland, who told me at a cocktail party that she definitely thought that was the color I should wear. When I remembered a beautiful *point d'esprit* headdress with floating flowers that I had seen once at Givenchy, I brazenly asked him if he would make this confection for the top of my head. He just smiled, and then dyed it to match the dress.

Hubert and Philippe Venet, his partner for over sixty-five years, would become my lifelong friends and travel companions. Hubert's homes, both in the country, which I write about in the next chapter, and his Paris house on Rue de Grenelle, were fascinating places of exceptional beauty that affected me nearly as much as his friendship and his couture.

Hubert lived in several extraordinary houses in Paris, but the one on Rue de Grenelle was magic. It was in a part of Paris near the Louvre where there were great seventeenth- and eighteenth-century houses that had survived the revolution and both world wars. He had a wonderful room with Boulle cabinets and modern paintings. I remember a dinner there with truffles in puff pastry served as a first course.

Hubert de Givenchy at Le Jonchet, 1977.

Hubert de Givenchy's apartment on Rue Fabert in Paris, 1978.

Deeda on the terrace of the Blairs' house in Washington, wearing a dress by Givenchy that was inspired by the Mark Rothko painting the designer had in his salon on Rue Fabert, 1972. Photo by Horst P. Horst for *Vogue*.

ON INSPIRATION

There was a very custom-made approach to life in Paris—from clothes to shoes and handbags to rooms and book binding—that appealed to me. I had a friend who painted her Mini to look like a basket and a favorite patisserie that made chocolate leaves and you could choose the type of tree the leaves came from. For me, Paris offered freedom and much to stimulate the imagination. It was a place where I could be immersed in history and museums and art galleries—and, of course, superb food. So, I decided to move there.

Mary Lasker
A Life in Science

Before moving to Paris, I stopped off in New York to attend a party for John F. Kennedy. There, I saw Bill, who invited me to join him the next night at a dinner at the home of his close friend Mary Lasker. In the entrance of Mary's house on Beekman Place, she had a large and unforgettable Matisse of plum blossoms. She also had one of two paintings by Van Gogh of white roses, paintings by Picasso and Braque, an amazing Cézanne, and in the dining room were nine more Matisses! I walked around as if in a trance. When I was leaving, Mary said, "I've never seen anyone look so intently at my collection. Would you like to come tomorrow for tea?"

That was the beginning of more than thirty years of a very close and fascinating friendship. As it turned out, we loved all the same things—Paris, gardens and houses, exhibitions, and biographies, histories, and books on art. Most importantly, Mary and I shared a deep interest in medical research. Eventually, we started traveling together twice-a-year to France, England, and occasionally to Italy. We would go to Paris for the couture collections, and then to the South of France,

where Mary rented Rory Cameron's house, the villa La Fiorentina, for the month of August. Bill and I would often stay with Mary in New York, and she would stay with us in Washington. Together we held dinners for senators and congressmen, frequently with a scientist speaking about exciting advances in research. Mary was a powerful force in the science world, and I think she recognized me as someone who shared this passion.

Mary was intent on creating a major public awareness campaign on high blood pressure, and so I arranged an appointment for us with Elliot Richardson, the secretary of health. I had met him the week before at a party at the British embassy where we had waltzed together. We briefed his deputy, and three weeks later, we had a lunch for Secretary Richardson and thirty CEOs and pharmaceutical executives who committed to Mary's idea of a national education campaign and promised significant financial support. Mary also enlisted the head of the Advertising Council to donate free advertising space on television, with celebrities and athletes appearing as spokespeople. The result was one of the most successful global public health initiatives ever launched, saving countless lives.

More than anyone I know, Mary worked toward finding a cure for cancer, in large part through the Lasker Foundation that she and her husband, Albert, set up. She also tirelessly lobbied members of the House and Senate health committees for public funds, and managed to substantially increase the congressional budget for the NIH year after year. The last time we spoke, when she was very ill just before she died, she talked to me about gene therapy and cancer vaccines. I learned so much from her. Her perseverance and commitment to her cause—you could call it zeal—was profoundly effective and was such an inspiration to so many people.

Mary Lasker with her beloved roses. Photo by Norman Parkinson.

One of the many wonderful paintings that hung in Mary Lasker's home on Beekman Place in New York:
Henri Matisse, *Méditation – Après le bain*, 1920. Oil on canvas. 28 ¾ x 21 ⅓ in. (73 x 54 cm).

Sarah Sze, *Shorter Than the Day*, 2020.
Powder-coated aluminum and steel.
48 x 30 x 30 ft. (1,463 x 914.4 x 914.4 cm).

John Singer Sargent, *Fumée d'ambre gris (Smoke of Ambergris)*, 1880.
Oil on canvas. 54 ¾ x 35 ¹¹⁄₁₆ in. (139.1 x 90.6 cm).

Mark Rothko, *Untitled*, 1970.
Oil on canvas. 68 x 54 in. (172.7 x 137.2 cm).

Anonymous, bust of Alexander the Great,
date unknown.

Raimundo de Madrazo y Garreta, *Woman in White*, c. 1880.
Oil on canvas. 28⅜ x 23⁹⁄₁₆ in. (72.1 x 59.8 cm).

Agnes Martin, *Untitled No. 1*, 1981.
Gesso, synthetic polymer paint, and pencil on canvas.
6 x 6 ft. (183 x 183 cm).

ON INSPIRATION

Agnolo Bronzino, *Portrait of Lucrezia Panciatichi*, c. 1545.
Oil on wood. 40 ⅛ x 34 ½ in. (102 x 85 cm).

Giovanni Domenico Tiepolo, *The Departure of the Gondola*, mid-1760s.
Oil on canvas. 14 ⅛ × 28 ¾ in. (35.9 × 73 cm).

Jacques Louis David, *Portrait of Antoine Laurent Lavoisier (1743–1794) and Marie Anne Lavoisier (Marie Anne Pierrette Paulze, 1758–1836)*, 1788. Oil on canvas. 102 ¼ x 76 ⅝ in. (259.7 x 194.6 cm).

ON INSPIRATION

Deeda tending her boxwood garden, which had four species of rare mini boxwood, just outside the dining room of her house in Washington, 2001. Photo by Eric Boman for *House Beautiful*.

Lulu de Waldner
A Love for Houses and Gardens

When I was living in Paris, a friend brought me to Lulu de Waldner's country house, La Grange, Mortefontaine, for lunch. Seeing it for the first time was like being deluged by imagination! The house was full of life and joy—a reflection of Lulu's own free spirit. It was like nothing I'd ever seen, and I adored it all. The garden was a bounty of flowers with a sense of fantasy, and the house was full of flowers, too—cut from her garden, printed on fabrics, and painted in pictures. There were objects everywhere in the shape of flowers and animals. There was not a decorator's hand in sight. Lulu found everything herself, riding all over Paris on a bicycle.

Lulu also had a remarkable house on Rue de Grenelle in Paris. Frequently, after an afternoon browsing Left Bank antique and book shops, I would visit for tea. There was a large drawing room that may have been the most attractive and comfortable room in Paris. On the walls she had a Le Manach red-and-cream cotton fabric of stripes and flowers, from which she had the flowers removed, leaving just the stripe. I have used it the same way, in blue-and-white silk gros de Naples, on the six Louis XVI chairs in my living room.

Every object in her home had a story behind it. One day, we were at a grand hotel for lunch, when she spotted a very tall gilt bronze candlestick sitting on the concierge desk. "I think I have the mate to that," she whispered to me. Lulu persuaded the manager to let her buy it. It turned out to be an exact match to her one very good eighteenth-century candlestick!

Even though her style was much more exuberant than my own, Lulu had a great influence on me.

She inspired me to have a deeply personal attitude toward decoration, and most importantly to pay attention to details and surround myself with things that bring joy.

Bill Blair
The Years in Politics

Bill visited me once while I was living in Paris and was shocked to learn that I wasn't planning to attend the 1960 Democratic convention. We were both very political, and he felt that I should be there. He managed to arrange a ride for me on a plane from London, and so I went to the convention.

After John F. Kennedy, or Jack, as we called him, was nominated as the candidate for the Democrats, I campaigned with Eunice, traveling with her and Jack to colleges across the Midwest. I also accompanied Rose, Jack and Eunice's mother, to tea party fundraisers all over Illinois. At a dinner the week of the inauguration, Jack said to me, "I think you should work at USIA [United States Information Agency]." Eunice's husband, Sarge, thought I should go to Health and Human Services, and Bobby Kennedy wanted me to work for the CIA (I loved that idea!).

Once Jack was in office, Bill became ambassador to Denmark, and before leaving for his post, he asked me to marry him. We were married in a beautiful ceremony at Frederiksborg Castle in Denmark, and the following year our son William was born. We loved Denmark. Bill visited the governor of every province in the country and almost every mayor. We had visits from numerous congressional delegations in the US, as well as former

Lulu de Waldner in her garden, Provence, 1990s. Photo by Derry Moore for *Architectural Digest*.

President John F. Kennedy, Deeda, and Bill in the Oval Office of the White House, Washington, D.C., early 1960s.

ON INSPIRATION

Deeda with her father on her wedding day, Frederiksborg Castle, Denmark, 1961. Her pale blue dress is by Balenciaga, the headdress is by Givenchy.

The newlywed Blairs at home in the embassy residence, Copenhagen, 1961.
They sit beneath René Bouché's portrait of Deeda.

The Blairs at La Fiorentina, 1962.

ON INSPIRATION

The lapidary garden, Villa Ephrussi de Rothschild, Saint-Jean-Cap-Ferrat, France.

A hornbeam-enclosed parterre of boxwood in Daniel Romualdez's garden, design by Miranda Brooks. Photo by Ngoc Minh Ngo.

Gerda Steiner & Jörg Lenzlinger, *Falling Garden* in San Staë church, Venice Biennale, 2003.

Japanese azaleas and dogwoods bloom in Babe Paley's garden at Kiluna Farm, design by Russell Page. Photo by Richard Champion.

Ruin of a neo-Gothic church.

Hornbeam hedges in Daniel Romualdez's garden,
design by Miranda Brooks. Photo by Ngoc Minh Ngo.

Sarah Sze, *Fallen Sky*, 2021.
Stainless steel. 44 x 432 x 432 in. (111.8 x 1,097.3 x 1,097.3 cm).
Storm King Art Center, New Windsor, New York.

ON INSPIRATION

President and Mrs. Eisenhower and even Vice President and Mrs. Nixon.

During each of four summers, I spent several weeks with Mary Lasker partaking in what I call "learning experiences," such as following David Karnovsky at Memorial Sloan Kettering on grand rounds. After seeing Mary, I would meet Bill in Paris, and together we would join Jayne and Charlie Wrightsman for trips on the Mediterranean with a stop to see Mary again, but this time at La Fiorentina.

After the death of President Kennedy, President Johnson appointed Bill to the Philippines. Life was more difficult in the Philippines. It was at the height of the war in Vietnam, and the related problems were frequently challenging. We were there for more than three years when Bobby Kennedy asked Bill to become the first general director of the still-under-construction Kennedy Center in Washington, D.C. That sounded very appealing—it meant American schools for William and a house of our own.

Bill found the perfect house for us, and we were so fortunate to have the help of Billy Baldwin with the decoration and Russell Page for the garden. We lived in that wonderful house for thirty-eight years. Bill was an extraordinary husband—so generous and thoughtful. I adored him—I don't think there was anyone who knew him who did not adore him.

Billy Baldwin
The Decoration of Houses

After living in embassy residences for so long, the house in Washington was the first home of our own. The only things we owned were six eighteenth-century painted chairs, Bill's collection of signed photographs, some antique porcelain, and an eighteenth-century *lit de repos*—a present from Bill that we chose instead of an engagement ring. In other words, nothing practical.

At the time, Billy Baldwin was at the height of his success, and he was hesitant about doing our house, as it was quite large and quite empty. But when we met, it was an immediate coming together of minds. Bill and Billy also became fast friends. Billy always arrived with only a small briefcase—no enormous tote stuffed with fabric samples! He would come only with what he thought would work.

Billy exercised restraint in his decoration, and encouraged it as well. During our first conversation, I told

him I had seen the most wonderful lacquer secretary in London. "I can already see that if it were up to you, you'd spend the whole budget on three things and have nothing left for the rest of the house," he said. "I don't think there will be any lacquer in this project now," he went on. "You must keep to your budget." Billy understood me, and really organized my thinking. If I found something on my own, he would be wildly enthusiastic. I knew I wasn't going to find antique Chinese wallpaper for our bedroom, so I decided on hand-painted curtains, for which Gracie & Company and I worked out a design of white flowers. Billy adored the idea, and suggested how they should be made.

Billy and Bill often discussed objects that I might like for Christmas, like blanc de chine inkwells or eighteenth-century botanical books. It was the era of the "tablescape"—that little landscape of artfully arranged objects on a table—which David Hicks took credit for, but which I think my friend Rory Cameron really started. The only time Bill put his foot down was when Billy and I wanted the darkest brown possible for the library. "No," Bill said. "We had to wear brown suits at Groton! No brown!" Bill wanted red walls for his library, an idea that both Billy and I thought was awful, but Billy convinced me that we should give in. A number of years later, we painted it a lovely stone color that we used again in New York.

Billy and I often shopped together. We went to Karl Springer, where we collaborated on the design of a two-tier tray side table that is now in my living room

Deeda at home, with Billy Baldwin at a party she hosted for his book *Billy Baldwin Remembers*, 1974.

Deeda at her home in Washington, D.C. designed by Billy Baldwin, 1972. Photo by Horst P. Horst for *Vogue*.

The Blairs' living room by Billy Baldwin, Washington, D.C., 1972. Photo by Horst P. Horst for *Vogue*.

Opposite: On the bureau is a faience camellia by Clare Potter, a tole
delphinium by Carmen Almon, and a real peony. The hand-painted curtains
are from France. Photo by Julia Hetta for *T Magazine*, the *New York Times*.

Deeda on vacation in Sicily, 1967. Photo by Cecil Beaton for *Vogue*.

in New York, and we would go to the furniture maker De Angelis, where Billy would sit on every sofa. He was a genius at stuffed sofas and chairs, for which he would find the perfect linens. We still have the pieces he made for us, and I still have things upholstered in exactly the same manner as he did—even transferring the passementerie Billy made onto newly upholstered pieces. He was also remarkable at the placement of furniture in a room, often saying that there is really only one great arrangement for every room. Everything Billy did was thoughtful and timeless, so there was never a need to rethink what he had done. When we downsized to an apartment in New York, I brought as much as I could possibly fit. I am lucky that Billy continues to linger in my life and home even though he is gone.

Jayne Wrightsman
The Eye Must Travel

In 1963, Mary Lasker brought Bill and me to a dinner at Jayne and Charlie Wrightsmans'. They were great philanthropists who would go on to donate an unparalleled collection to the Metropolitan Museum of Art. Jayne's generosity was thoughtful and visionary, a fact made most clear by the Wrightsman Galleries at the Met, which are filled with her collection of eighteenth-century French decorative arts, and are among the finest period rooms in the world. Jayne was a self-taught expert in eighteenth-century decorative arts and old master paintings. She had an insatiable curiosity, and was highly disciplined, with the probing mind of a scholar. I don't think I've ever been as awestruck as when I first saw the paintings she had in her New York apartment. They were of a quality you see only in museums, and yet there was nothing stiff about these rooms where one sat among Rubens, Vermeer, the Gerard David *Madonna*, and Van Dyck's *Henrietta Maria*. In the dining room, Jayne had an easel supporting a rare Boilly depicting visitors to the Louvre looking at Jacques Louis David's painting of the coronation of Napoleon. There were magnificent drawings in the gallery and a collection of Ingres portraits that was breathtaking. Until the end of her life, Jayne collected old master paintings and drawings with knowledge and passion, and a commitment to gifting them to the Met.

Her legendary taste extended to all aspects of her life: her clothes, her flowers, her writing paper, her tone of voice, and the meals she served. I'll never forget a luncheon in Palm Beach of asparagus followed by cold roast chicken packed with foie gras, and then for dessert a crisp pastry sculpted into a demitasse cup filled with coffee mousse. The tables she did for an opening night dinner at the Met were among my all-time favorites: enchanting bird cages made of boxwood were filled with her collection of eighteenth-century Meissen birds, a few of which had "escaped" and made their way down the oval tables.

Jayne and I seemed to become friends immediately. I would see her most often in France, where we would go on excursions to places like Chantilly, Fontainbleu, or Vaux Le Vicomte, or to out of the way lesser known places. She was an obsessive sightseer, as was I. We both loved biographies and collections of letters, and almost every week, she would send me a book. Thanks to Jayne, I began to read intensively about eighteenth-century France.

Bill and I went on four glorious Mediterranean voyages with the Wrightsmans on the *Radiant*. Trips with them were highly organized and well-curated affairs, with detailed itineraries arriving in leather-bound dossiers in the spring. There was always a rotating cast of friends in attendance, as well as museum directors, curators, and academics, and people like Cecil Beaton, Katharine Graham, Kenneth Clark, and Margaret and Johnnie Walker. One summer we sailed down the Dalmatian coast and ended up in Capri and Naples. Another year we began in Istanbul, then meandered over to Israel, Lebanon, Samothrace, and Corsica.

After Charlie died, Jayne sold their house in Palm Beach and divided her time between New York and London. In addition to porcelain and paintings, Jayne continued to collect rare books with wonderful engraved

Jayne Wrightsman, 1963. Photo by Cecil Beaton for *Vogue*.

ON INSPIRATION

Bill attending an event as US ambassador of the
Philippines, mid- to late 1960s.

Deeda and Bill at Tivoli Gardens the night before their wedding,
Copenhagen, Denmark, 1961.

The Blairs in Isfahan, Iran, early 1970s.

Above and below left: The Blairs "roughing it" in Antumalal, Chile, 1960s.

Bill in Novosibirsk, Siberia, late 1950s.

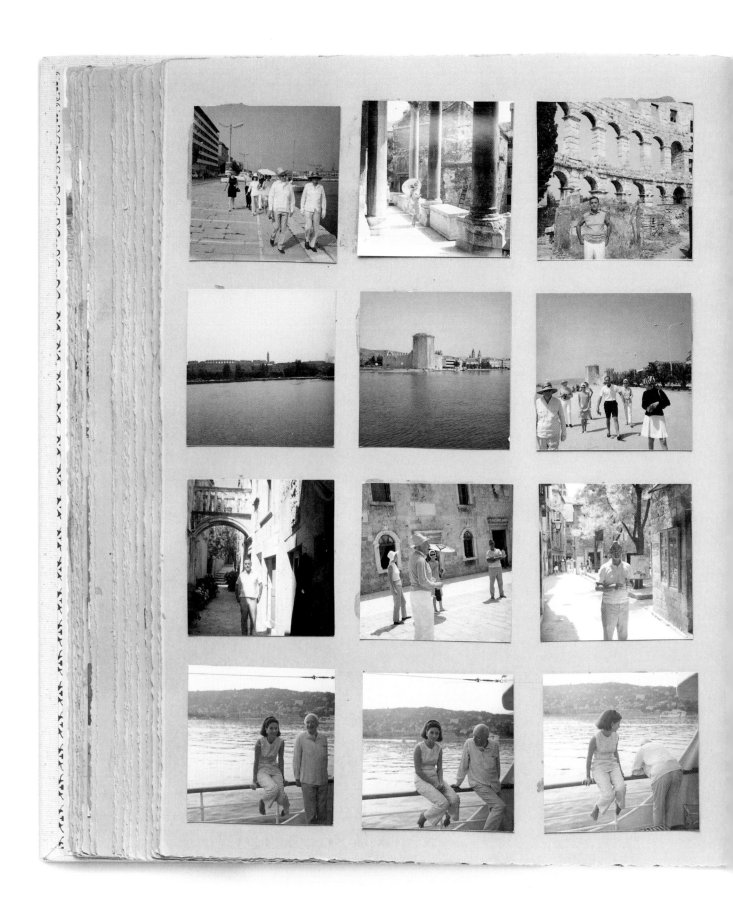

Snapshots from one of Deeda's scrapbooks showing her and Bill with the Wrightsmans and friends traveling in the Mediterranean on the *Radiant*, late 1960s.

guess who?

Jeeda   Cecil Beaton

illustrations, many originally made for royal families, and bound by the most renowned binders of their day. She also continued to travel, and for five summers we traversed Germany by car, taking lovely country roads to museums, palaces, and libraries.

Jayne's generosity extended beyond the world of art. Few are aware that in the mid-1980s the Wrightsmans gave the very first MRI scanner to New York Hospital, initiating a new era of imaging diagnostics. As was typical of Jayne, modesty prevailed and there were no dedications or names engraved on plaques or publicity around this momentous gift—underlying the generosity there was always discretion.

I was fortunate to be a part of so many wonderful times and inspiring journeys filled with laughter, art, books, wonderful food, and magnificent sights.

My Working Life

By the time William was in his twenties and Bill had retired, my working life changed in a number of significant ways. I had been working with Mary Lasker on her foundation for nearly 30 years—a mixture of attending seminars and meetings, visiting researchers and learning about groundbreaking discoveries. I had also served on the boards of Scripps Research Institute, the American Cancer Society research committee, the Foundation for the NIH, and had been involved with the Harvard School of Public Health for more than three decades, which led to my long connection with the Harvard AIDS Institute.

During that time, I made many friends in the pharmaceutical and biotech industries, and then Dr. Max Link, the American president of Sandoz, a pharmaceutical company, invited me to consult for them. I had never worked in the private sector, but now I helped bring

top scientific researchers together with biotech companies and institutes with the goal of developing new health care solutions for cancer and other diseases.

Later, a friend from Johnson & Johnson, who was forming a venture capital group focused on health care, asked me to help build "the best scientific advisory board," to review the latest research. Five companies, including one devoted to gene therapy, came out of that first committee we assembled. Over the next twenty years I became a senior advisor for eighteen different companies, and I found it gratifying and fulfilling to be working with so many innovative scientists. I was very lucky that Bill was so supportive of my work through the years.

After our much-loved son, William, who had struggled with depression and bipolar disorder for years, committed suicide at age 41, I began to dedicate myself to advancing research in the study of the brain. I had always been interested in the biology of the brain, partly because it is the most complicated and fascinating organ in the human body, but also because mental health research had always lagged behind cancer and other diseases in funding. Now that Bill too, is gone, having died in 2015, raising funds and awarding research grants to innovative physician-scientists administered by the Deeda Blair Research Initiative for Disorders of the Brain has become my primary focus (see page 250).

When I'm not working on the Initiative, I never tire of reading, looking at art, or being with friends for dinner in an apartment I love that reflects my life. This book brings together all of my passions: sharing the recipes I adore and the people, places, and art that inspire me. It is also my hope that it will raise awareness and funds, in honor of my son, for innovative scientific research to encourage collaboration and spread new thoughts and ideas.

Deeda with Dr. Max Essex at a medical conference in Japan, 1980s.

PART II

FANTASY MENUS

78   Lunch at Haga Pavilion, Sweden

92   Sunday Lunch at La Fiorentina, Italy

106   Picnic on a Visit to Egyptian Treasures, US

118   Luncheon at Château du Jonchet, France

134   Dinner at Pavlovsk Palace, Russia

146   Dinner at the Petit Trianon, France

Solna, Sweden

LUNCH AT HAGA PAVILION

I once visited Sweden on a private tour of Swedish manor houses and castles that was organized by the Georgian Group of London. I went with two close friends—Michael Mahoney, an art historian, and Raymond Bahor, a doctor at NIH. It was after William had died, and Michael and Raymond were among the few people I felt comfortable being with during that awful time. They are passionate sightseers, low key, with a dry sense of humor.

Traveling all over the Swedish countryside, we saw many wonderful places, among them the Palladian house Elghammar designed by Quarenghi, one of Catherine the Great's favorite architects. At Drottningholm, we were fascinated by the huge palace, but for me it was the Chinese pavilion in the garden there that was pure magic. I adored the simplicity and restraint of Swedish neo-classicism, the painted furniture and carpetless floors, as well as the Swedish reverence for nature, as seen in the well-kept gardens and flowering meadows. I was totally transported by everything we saw.

But the Haga Pavilion, just outside Stockholm, affected me in a way few places ever have. It was a revelation. Gustav III fell in love with the Haga estate when he was crown prince, and when he became king he bought it as a refuge of quiet serenity and privacy away from his official duties. He designed the pavilion in 1787, in the neoclassical style inspired by the then-recent excavations of the ancient Roman remains at Pompeii and Herculaneum.

The facade of the pavilion is simple and austere, without ornament, so the first impression is one of great understatement. But once inside, you progress through an enfilade of rooms, lavishly decorated in the Pompeiian style. Your eye is carried along from room to room by two magnificent crystal chandeliers that hang in each, until suddenly you arrive at the final room, the Hall of Mirrors. This space was nothing short of breathtaking. Fashioned almost entirely of mirrors and large glass windows supported by columns, everything in it was utterly perfect in scale and proportion. Just beyond the windows, the romantic English-style landscape, with its lake and magnificent trees, opened out. I now know this room is considered one of the most beautiful neoclassical rooms in all of Europe, but none of us knew anything about it before visiting, and so we came upon it without preconceptions. There is no question that it is one of the most imaginative rooms I have ever seen. It possessed an atmosphere that made us never want to leave.

As king, Gustave III was a patron of literature and the arts, and held readings and small theatricals in the pavilion. He was also a great collector, traveling to Italy often to acquire antiquities; a personal tour by Pope Pius VI

Previous spread: View of the Hall of Mirrors from the park at Haga Pavilion, built by Olof Tempelman for King Gustav III, 1788. The surrounding park was designed by Fredrik Magnus Piper.

of the ancient sculptures at the Vatican had a great influence on his taste.
He had begun to lay the foundation for a magnificent palace on the estate
that would hold these works, when he was assassinated at a masquerade
ball by a conspiracy of princes angered by his reforms. (Gustav III was a
complex figure who married the ideals of democracy with a penchant for
autocracy and extravagance.) The following year, in 1793, his antiquity
collection was installed in the Royal Palace in Stockholm, where it remains
today in precisely the same configuration as in the eighteenth century.
The palace was later completed and is now home to Crown Princess Victoria.
But it is the extraordinary pavilion, beautifully preserved with much of
its original decoration intact, and open to the public in the summer, which
is his masterpiece.

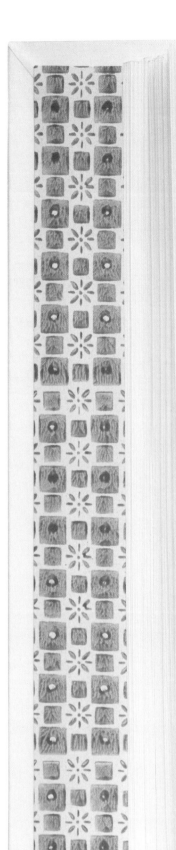

Clockwise from top left: A folly on the Haga estate; the large salon in Haga Pavilion; Gustav III's collection of ancient sculpture at the Museum of Antiquities in the Royal Palace in Stockholm; the library in Haga Pavilion.

Following spread: The Hall of Mirrors, Haga Pavilion.

HAGA PAVILION

50

LUNCH AT HAGA PAVILION

FIRST COURSE
Cold Vegetables
with Herbs and Vinaigrette

MAIN COURSE
Harissa-Marinated Chicken
with Grapefruit Salad
and
Fried Potato Ribbons

DESSERT
Green Grape Mold
with Custard Sauce

A table set for a fantasy meal inspired by Deeda's memories of the colors of
Sweden and the light and airy atmosphere of Haga Pavilion. Photo by Ngoc Minh Ngo.

My dream would be to have a picnic inspired by Haga's luminous atmosphere. The Swedish palette is often pale and soft, with blues, whites, creams, and grays—never anything garish. But to me, blue and white are the colors of Sweden. In Stockholm, we often ate at a restaurant that had a menu edged with a patterned garland in various shades of blue and white, which I have never forgotten.

So, I chose a Bennison tablecloth in the Roses pattern. I had it made in a pale grayish blue with white, which reminds me of the natural beauty and love of flowers that inspire the Swedish imagination. Under the tablecloth's ruffled bottom edge is another fabric in blue and white gingham, which also feels very Swedish. To blue and white, I like to add a bit of pink. In my garden in Washington, I planted only white and pale pink roses. So, for the flowers here, we added some pink roses and lilacs to the palette.

For this meal, I started with a simple cold vegetable dish with herbs in homage to the many wonderful vegetable gardens we saw in Sweden. At the restaurant we frequented, I had chicken with a spiciness that reminds me of the chicken with harissa that is the main course of this menu. I chose the dessert of green grapes in a mold because, while simple, it is also quite special. Its pale green recalls the color of spring, and its shimmering translucency reminds me of the glass and mirrors in the Hall of Mirrors at Haga that I so adored.

It would also be great fun to imagine holding a party in the Hall of Mirrors using this tablecloth of roses. Of course, we'd all have to get very dressed up in white dresses . . .

Cold Vegetables with Herbs and Vinaigrette on page 173.
Harissa-Marinated Chicken with Grapefruit Salad on page 194.
Fried Potato Ribbons on page 210.
Green Grape Mold with Custard Sauce on page 232.

Harissa-marinated chicken with grapefruit salad, fried potato ribbons, and a side bowl of harissa served on Deeda's plates made in Apt, France, on a custom-colored tablecloth by Bennison. Photo by Ngoc Minh Ngo.

Green Grape Mold

Opposite: Deeda's dining table by the window overlooking the
East River in her Manhattan living room. Photo by Ngoc Minh Ngo.

SUNDAY LUNCH AT LA FIORENTINA

Rory Cameron was one of the most interesting men I have ever met. He was born into a family of wealth and curiosity—both intellectual and aesthetic. Rory's mother, the legendary Lady Enid, Countess of Kenmare, led a life of immense luxury and had four husbands and many lovers. Travel was a constant in their lives. Rory was educated in many different countries—France, Egypt, England, Germany—and he wrote several books, mostly about travel. As a child, he lived in Egypt with his mother, and in 1947, he wrote of a remarkable voyage, beginning in Paris, going on to Chantilly, Malta, and finally to the Mena House Hotel near the pyramids at Giza. Rory felt it impossible to describe the extraordinary scale of the pyramids. He told me once that his favorite memory was of being among the first, at only eight years old, to be taken down to see King Tutankhamun's tomb after it was discovered in 1922.

Rory was different from his family, as he was modest and had a subtle sense of humor. He was interested in people—intriguing social figures, intellectuals, and writers—and in art, architecture, and interior design. His passion was for beauty, and the breadth of his knowledge and the originality of his imagination entranced me.

In 1939, his mother's third husband, Lord Furness, purchased a large property at the tip of Saint-Jean-Cap-Ferrat in southern France, which included an immense Italianate villa called La Fiorentina that was later badly damaged by the Germans during the Second World War. A summer spent traveling and sightseeing in Italy after the war inspired Rory to rebuild La Fiorentina in the manner of La Rotonda, the great Palladian villa near Venice.

You approached the villa through a double allée of fragrant orange trees with whitewashed trunks, arriving at the discreet but splendid staircase to the house, which was always edged with pots of clipped boxwoods. After passing through the entry hall with trompe l'oeil murals painted by Martin Battersby, you entered a vast living room where every piece of furniture seemed to be in the ideal position to facilitate comfort, conversation, and dogs. Rory had a gifted sense for the placement of furniture, believing that it must "fall well" into its most natural location.

Rory hated bright colors, so on the walls he used a pale shade of silver that mimicked the underside of an olive leaf, along with pale yellows and creams, all of which provided a perfect background for his furniture, paintings, sculptures, and gilded mirrors. The room gave onto a terrace with oversized lounges facing the sea. Beyond the terrace, a pair of French stone sphinxes—one was said to have the head of Madame de Pompadour and the other of Madame du Barry—

Previous spread: A view of the Mediterranean from the back of La Fiorentina, Saint-Jean-Cap-Ferrat on the French Riviera. Photo by Durston Saylor for *Architectural Digest*.

flanked the top of a long set of wide, shallow grass steps bordered by columnar cypresses. The steps led to a very narrow, very long pool—quite likely the first "infinity" pool, whose water spilled into the sea. The gardens of La Fiorentina were magical, with masses of olive trees and very subtle sweeps of Mediterranean plants. He made a vine-covered loggia where we always had lunch, and a one-room building where he did his writing. Inside the villa, Rory designed a master suite for the summer and another for the winter, as well as several large guest suites.

I met Rory during my first visit to La Fiorentina with Mary Lasker, who rented the villa every August for fifteen years in the 1960s and 1970s. For most of those years, I joined her. That first time, Mary was giving a luncheon for Princess Grace of Monaco, and I was seated next to Rory. I had noticed about twenty very large scrapbooks on his bookshelves and asked him if I might look at them. He charmingly said, "Yes, but don't try to lift them as they are fiercely heavy, and read them in the library where the others won't see you. I don't want everyone going through them." The books were filled with marvelous photographs of gardens, people, houses, landscapes, and works of art—a mix of places and things he loved.

I was inspired to do something like this myself, and began collecting images, mostly from magazines. Eventually, during a quiet period, I organized the images by subject, laid them all out, and had them bound in vellum.

Another time, I asked Rory if when he rents the house, he puts certain of his treasures away. He smiled and said, "Yes, I'll show you." I followed him into a guest room upstairs, where he opened a large jib door hidden in the wall to reveal shelves filled with porcelains, small paintings, rare drawings, pottery, and sculpture of all kinds. He said, "You must have something for the desk in your room," and gave me a clay fragment of an ancient Egyptian ceramic wig that had been glazed a brilliant turquoise. Another year, he gave me a fourth-century BCE terracotta Tanagra figurine for my room.

Over time, the South of France became much more crowded—more houses, more people, and horrific traffic. Rory sold La Fiorentina and moved to Provence, where he built his last house, Les Quatre Sources, and filled it with the books and treasures of his lifetime.

Clockwise from top left: The facade of La Fiorentina. Photo by Durston Saylor for *Architectural Digest*; the dining terrace at La Fiorentina. Photo by Durston Saylor for *Vogue*; the whitewashed orange trees at the entrance.

44

Clockwise from top left: An ancient terracotta statuette of a goddess; Rory Cameron and Deeda at Chatsworth, 1970s; the dining room at La Fiorentina decorated with eighteenth-century Piedmontese oil-on-canvas wall coverings. Photo by Durston Saylor for *Architectural Digest*; Rory's mother, Enid, Countess of Kenmare, 1937.

51

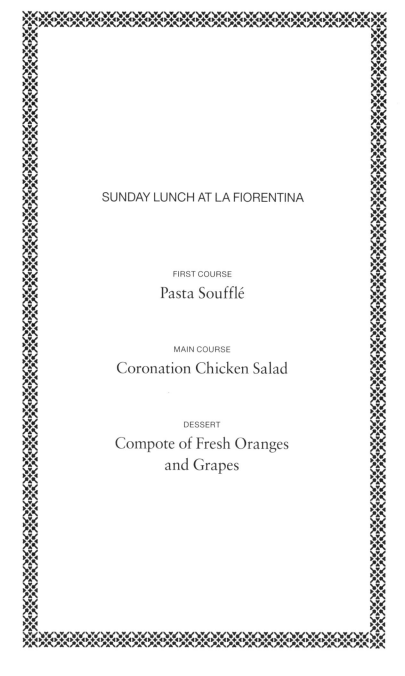

SUNDAY LUNCH AT LA FIORENTINA

FIRST COURSE
Pasta Soufflé

MAIN COURSE
Coronation Chicken Salad

DESSERT
Compote of Fresh Oranges
and Grapes

Opposite: To evoke the feeling of Rory Cameron's La Fiorentina, Deeda opted for a
muted neutral palette with only white flowers and citrus adorning an uncovered table.
The pasta soufflé is served individually in rattan-covered ramekins. Photo by Ngoc Minh Ngo.

Following spread: The Jansen table is set for lunch in a pared-back style
reminiscent of meals on the loggia at La Fiorentina. Photo by Ngoc Minh Ngo.

MENU NOTES

During the time that Rory would stay with Mary and me at La Fiorentina, he would plan our menus, as he loved food. His cook was a delightful woman who arrived every morning from Villefranche on a bicycle with a large basket filled with strawberries, peaches, figs, and baguettes. What came out of her kitchen was delicious—always wonderfully simple and perfectly prepared. Rory's tables were simple as well—no tablecloths and no flowers—but often with a few pieces from his amazing collection of English and French porcelain and charming pottery, mostly from the region of Apt. He also had a group of Picasso plates that he frequently used.

For this menu, in honor of Rory, I went with a pared back, tonal palette for the plates and dishes, and since I never set a table without flowers, I used only white flowers. To create a more masculine look, I used my steel Jansen table that is usually in the window of the library, pulling it out and adding leaves to extend it, but I left it uncovered.

I tried to include dishes in my menu for Rory that are somewhat out of the ordinary and perhaps even surprising, so the first course is a pasta soufflé of my own invention, which I have never had anywhere else. We use tagliolini, because they are narrow, thin, and very light.

The next course is my version of Rory's coronation chicken recipe, which he often served. We add a small amount of apricot preserves to the homemade curried mayonnaise. I serve this dish with three small lacquered bowls that contain thinly sliced green bananas, sliced almonds, and chutney that people can add to the salad if they like.

The dessert is a simple compote of sliced fresh navel oranges and grapes sprinkled with a Cointreau syrup that reminds me of the fragrant orange trees and vine-covered pergola at La Fiorentina.

Pasta Soufflé on page 185.
Coronation Chicken Salad on page 182.
Compote of Fresh Oranges and Grapes on page 230.

Rory's coronation chicken salad served with bananas, almonds, and chutney on the side.

PICNIC ON A VISIT TO EGYPTIAN TREASURES

After not having traveled in quite some time because of back issues, my friends Anastasia Vournas and Bill Uhrig generously offered to whisk me away to anywhere I wanted. When I said my dream was to go to St. Louis, they were at first rather surprised, and then delighted when I told them that one of the most important archaeological discoveries of the last thousand years was traveling to the Saint Louis Art Museum. *Sunken Cities: Egypt's Lost Worlds* was an exhibition of many treasures excavated from two ancient, incredibly sophisticated Egyptian cites, Thonis and Canopus, which had been buried beneath the sea near Alexandria for centuries. Once thriving centers of trade between Egypt, Greece, and the wider Mediterranean, by the eighth century, the cities were submerged by floods and tidal waves, where they remained hidden and forgotten until late in the twentieth century.

I had seen part of this exhibition in Paris when it opened at the Grand Palais in 2006, and was longing to see it again. Once the destination and date were settled, we invited our great mutual friends Harold Koda, Alan Kornberg, and Anne Goldrach. Bill flies his own plane, and I offered to bring a picnic for the ride. Terence Eagleton, a really thoughtful friend from St. Louis, went ahead to organize everything for us. When we arrived, Terence took us to see many beautiful old houses and to Tadao Ando's building for the Pulitzer Arts Foundation. That evening Terence gave a very festive dinner where he arranged the tables with white peonies and maidenhair ferns, which he knew I adored. Early the next morning, we were off to the exhibit, where we spent nearly four hours spellbound.

There were remarkable sculptures, vessels, and jewelry. Among all the wonderful things we saw, three monumental granite sculptures—of a pharaoh, a queen, and a god, each nearly eighteen feet high, that had once guarded the entrance to a temple—took our breath away. But my absolute favorite thing was a mesmerizing statue of the Egyptian queen Arsinoe II from the third century BCE. It was carved from dark stone in a rigid frontal posture that felt entirely Egyptian, but the sensual rendering of the flesh and the naturalistic folds of the drapery were masterfully Greek. In it, you can see the rich commingling of styles between Egypt and Greece at that time. Here, Arsinoe is represented as the Greek goddess Aphrodite, as she was revered by both Egyptians and Greeks despite her rather complicated personal history. At fifteen, she married the sixty-year-old King Lysimachus, but when she grew concerned about succession after one of her sons had a son of his own, she had her young grandson poisoned. When Lysimachus died, Arsinoe went on to marry her half-brother. When things soured between them, she plotted with her sons against him. But he got there first, killing two of her three sons. After that, Arsinoe married her full brother. She went on to share in all of her brother-husband's titles and ruled influentially alongside him, remaining popular throughout the Ptolemaic period among both Egyptians and Greeks. For centuries—after being conquered by Alexander the Great and until the Roman Empire—Greeks and Egyptians lived side by side, sharing their cultures, beliefs, and customs. The discovery of these cities shed new light on these joined histories, all of which can be witnessed in this one magnificent work of art.

To see the remains of a shipwreck with artifacts is one thing, but to see the remains of entire ancient cities, their treasures brought to the surface once again, was an extraordinary experience.

The exhibition *Sunken Cities: Egypt's Lost Worlds* at the Saint Louis Art Museum in 2016 included many of the treasures painstakingly retrieved from beneath the sea, off the coast of Egypt, by archaeologists led by Franck Goddio. From left to right: A statue of a queen, probably Cleopatra II or III, from the Ptolemaic period, fourth century BCE, discovered by Goddio; a statue of Arsinoe II; the same statue being brought from the sea.

36

Deeda's snapshots from the exhibition *Sunken Cities: Egypt's Lost Worlds* at the Saint Louis Art Museum, 2016.
The figures seen opposite are nearly eighteen feet high.

EGYPTIAN TREASURES

PICNIC ON A VISIT
TO EGYPTIAN TREASURES

FIRST COURSE
Deeda's Cold Beet Soup

MAIN COURSE
Moroccan Chicken and Couscous

DESSERT
Blueberry and Blackberry Tart

This wonderful combination of colorful dishes works as well for a meal on
the go as for a bright and easy lunch at home. Photo by Ngoc Minh Ngo.

Deeda's Cold Beet Soup

MENU NOTES

For our trip, I brought along a picnic that was packed up in a few wicker baskets with some bamboo flatware and gingham napkins, which felt appropriately casual for a lunch on the go. I am always on the lookout for attractive baskets, mostly made of willow or rush, and I use them for storing everything at home, also as containers for potted plants.

I selected this menu because everything could be served cold or at room temperature, and it is all easy to eat and not messy. But I also chose these recipes because the dishes are unusual, well liked, and very colorful. The deep rose of the beet soup, the mixed hues of the chicken with couscous, and the jewel tones of the dark blueberry and blackberry tart with its shiny glaze all look so attractive together. My fried Anastasia brought along thermoses from Germany, so we each had an individual container of the icy cold beet soup. After we got back to the hotel, a few people asked if there was any more soup—it is one of my most requested recipes.

Deeda's Cold Beet Soup on page 167.
Moroccan Chicken and Couscous on page 184.
Blueberry and Blackberry Tart on page 224.

LUNCHEON AT CHÂTEAU DU JONCHET

When Hubert de Givenchy was at the height of his career, he was not inclined to be part of *tout Paris* and go to parties. He was very disciplined: up early, often arriving at his atelier before anyone else, returning home for lunch most days, and then back to work. He was building his business with accessories and perfumes, and was among the first to launch wonderful high-end ready-to-wear.

He lived in a number of different apartments and houses in Paris in those years, all of which were wonderful. It was a joy to be in his rooms, full as they were of the magnificent things he had begun to collect, like Renaissance bronzes, Boulle furniture, and Limoges enamels. He liked to entertain only one or two people at a time, and the lunches he served were always delicious.

For many years, Bill and I would see Hubert and his partner, Philippe Venet, in Venice, as they went every summer at the same time we did. One day in the 1970s, Hubert told me that he had fallen in love with a *maison de campagne*, and that it was the house of his dreams. Le Jonchet was a remarkably beautiful seventeenth-century château with a large forest along a river. I didn't visit for a few years, as there was much that needed to be done for it to reach his standards.

When the time came, I was mesmerized by its staggering beauty. The buildings were symmetrical and made of a lovely pale stone with very tall windows that filled the interiors with light. The house was still somewhat unfinished, but Hubert and Philippe had each taken a vast room to make glorious ateliers for themselves. Hubert's had a very large blue Miró and a few large worktables for researching and sketching—it had a perfect sense of emptiness about it. Philippe's was filled with books and wicker chairs and baskets everywhere, rather like mine at home but with less disorder. Most of the furniture was comfortable upholstered chairs and sofas, and there were several Diego Giacometti tables and benches.

It wasn't until he retired that Hubert began to entertain more frequently at home. But even during those years, he guarded his privacy, and when I visited Jonchet, I would often be the only guest for the weekend. On Saturday, Hubert served a largish lunch and a light supper. During the day, we took long walks through the gardens and woods. There was something new to see each time, as he was always improving things. When he and his great friend Bunny Mellon were restoring the Potager du Roi at Versailles, he found a stag's head and had several copies of it made for Versailles, and then a few more made for the facade at Jonchet.

Previous spread: In homage to Hubert de Givenchy's château in France, Deeda used a pale palette, eighteenth-century French bowls, a tablecloth reminiscent of the garden, and her set of Louis XVI chairs covered in a delicate checked taffeta embroidered in muslin. Photo by Ngoc Minh Ngo.

Hubert adored gardens, and he studied every aspect of them carefully with Bunny. She was often there with him, discussing ideas and improvements in an atmosphere of quiet and tranquility. Over time, they redid his gardens, creating a large potager and a rose garden with woven wattle fencing. There was one existing garden next to the house that had been done in the French style of the nineteenth century with lots of ordinary flowers. Hubert had so admired a parterre garden at the Cini Foundation in Venice, in the cloister of the monastery at San Giorgio, that he asked permission to copy it—plant for plant, centimeter by centimeter. It consisted of a series of concentric boxwood circles, some circles inside of others, all cut very low (just a few inches high), set in grass, and surrounded by a boxwood "hedge" that was only a few inches higher. The original monastery garden was completed in the seventeenth century—Palladio had designed the cloister—and yet it felt so modern in its abstract geometry. That Italian garden was a triumph at Jonchet, and as with all Hubert did, it seemed almost inevitable.

While the beauty and grandeur of his last Paris house on Rue de Grenelle was amazing—with its gilded furniture, silks, and velvets—Jonchet was equally marvelous in its monumental and ultra-sophisticated simplicity. It was so airy and light, with white linen slipcovers and upholstery, and yet at the same time, it was elevated to a state of perfection. Like Rory, Hubert knew intuitively where furniture should fall in a room; he had that same sense for putting things in just the right place.

From left to right: Deeda in one of the bedrooms at Jonchet. Snapshot by Philippe Venet;
a pale palette dominates furnishings throughout the rooms at Jonchet. Photo by Dylan Thomas.

Previous spread: A bronze stag by François Pompon dominates one of the salons at Jonchet.
Photo by Dylan Thomas.

CHÂTEAU DU JONCHET

Clockwise from top left: Jonchet's facade features stags' heads based on one Givenchy had found.
Photo by Dylan Thomas; Givenchy fell in love with a boxwood garden in Venice and recreated it at
Jonchet. Photo by Pablo Zamora; Givenchy's atelier at Jonchet. Photo by Pablo Zamora.

CHÂTEAU DU JONCHET

LUNCHEON AT CHÂTEAU DU JONCHET

FIRST COURSE
Deeda's Iced Cauliflower Soup
with Crisp Croutons

MAIN COURSE
Gruyère Roulade

DESSERT
Anela's Poached Fresh Apple
with Walnuts and Honey

Deeda's cauliflower soup with croutons and frisée on a two-piece
tablecloth set with pleated edges by Bennison. Photo by Ngoc Minh Ngo.

MENU NOTES

In thinking about the table and menu for Hubert, there was no point in even trying for an appearance similar to his. His cupboards were full of eighteenth-century silver and porcelain tureens, rare plates, and the most beautiful glasses made in Venice. So, I thought I must go in a different direction, but that I would keep the overall feeling very light and airy.

I moved the table away from the window, where it usually sits, and into the center of the living room, so that it seemed to float in the emptiness of space—a quality Hubert might appreciate. I had just had a lovely round flowered silk tablecloth made with a pleated flounce at the hem and an additional square cloth to go on top. Then, to add even more flowers, and to recall his woven garden fence, I used my eighteenth-century plates with a basket edge.

The flowers for the table were done by my friend Cathy Graham, who used all pale tones, but with something unexpected: a deep black center in the white anemones, a soft red picotee on the edges of the ranunculus, and the slender branches of a dogwood tree with a delicate blue clematis weaving itself through the arrangement. Cathy's sense of the romantic is subtle and imaginative and suited the table to perfection.

Hubert was interested in food and loved when dishes were surprising. I remember once he served as a first course a pyramid of fresh individual truffles covered with puff pastry that was almost too heavenly to describe. Everyone gracefully declined when it was passed a second time, except me, and when I took another serving, everyone else changed their minds. So, we tried to have a little of the unexpected in our menu as well.

I decided on a cauliflower soup recipe that is unusual. I make it with finely chopped cauliflower topped with a bouquet of frisée lettuce and small croutons. To make the soup very cold, just before serving I throw in a tablespoon of tiny ice chips. This gives it an unexpected crunch.

The second course is a cheese roulade, which is like a cheese soufflé that has been flattened and wrapped around a salad. The dessert is a specialty from Anela, who came from Montenegro to work for me. It is a poached whole apple, simple and delicious, with a sauce made by reducing the poaching liquid.

Deeda's Iced Cauliflower Soup with Crisp Croutons on page 164.
Gruyère Roulade on page 178.
Anela's Poached Fresh Apple with Walnuts and Honey on page 230.

Previous spread: To evoke the feeling of monumental simplicity that Givenchy achieved in his interiors at Le Jonchet, Deeda moved her dining table in front of the bare lacquered wall of her living room with its simple Corinthian-topped pilasters. Photo by Ngoc Minh Ngo.

Opposite: Anela's apple and walnut dessert on the table with men's handkerchiefs from the Parisian shirt maker Charvet, which Deeda uses as napkins, and French Aptware demitasse cups with black-and-white marbling. Photo by Ngoc Minh Ngo.

St. Petersburg, Russia

DINNER AT PAVLOVSK PALACE

The story of the great palace at Pavlovsk is one of creation, destruction, and heroic restoration. The palace is the finest example of neoclassical architecture in Russia and embodies the deep culture and complicated history of Russia itself. In 1777, Catherine the Great gave her son, Paul I, and his wife 800 acres south of St. Petersburg, ostensibly to celebrate the birth of their first son, but also to get Paul I out of her way, as she was not terribly fond of him. It was his wife, the German-Alsatian princess and later empress, Maria Feodorovna, who influenced and oversaw every aspect of the palace's construction and decoration. Her ability to mix important French pieces with priceless antiquities and handcrafted Russian furniture was nothing short of amazing. So beautiful was the palace that even the Bolsheviks chose to preserve rather than ransack it. But during the Second World War, it was burned to the ground. Afterward, the Russians decided to rebuild it, brick by brick, an unfathomable feat that took nearly fifty years.

I came to know and love the palace through Hélène de Ludinghausen, who was the last of a storied Russian aristocratic family, the Stroganoffs, and had grown up in exile in Paris. She spent thirty years as *directrice* of Yves Saint Laurent Couture, before deciding in 1992 to set up the Stroganoff Foundation to create a cultural exchange program between Russia and the United States. Hélène sought to raise funds for the preservation of some of Russia's important cultural sites—Stroganoff Palace, Pavlovsk, Gatchina, the Hermitage—and organized a number of exclusive, invitation-only trips to St. Petersburg for friends and museum curators. I went on her tours four times, and each time Pavlovsk was more restored, and more magnificent, than the last.

Maria Feodorovna went through four eminent architects before she was done, but the palace building itself was the work of Catherine the Great's architect Charles Cameron, who was inspired by Palladio's plans for the Villa Rotonda in Venice. Pavlovsk is restrained in its design, with a central cube-shaped building supported by dozens of columns and flanked on each side by elegantly curved, low-storied colonnaded wings. The surrounding park was done in the English style. Maria Feodorovna took great inspiration from her travels with her husband through France, Italy, Austria, and Germany, where they went about under the pseudonym "the Count and Countess of the North." At Versailles, Louis XVI gave them four Gobelins tapestries and Marie Antoinette gave them a sixty-piece set of Sèvres porcelain.

Maria Feodorovna made Pavlovsk a showcase for the finest eighteenth-century French craftsmanship. The Rose Pavilion, where we had dinner on my

Previous spread: Pavlovsk Palace in winter is breathtaking.

last visit, was built early in the nineteenth century and surrounded entirely with rose bushes. Later, she commissioned a library for her collection of 20,000 books and a lavender room painted in lilac-colored scagliola to match the blooms outside.

Just before the German attack on Russia in June of 1941, the curators of Pavlovsk began carefully packing up its most precious objects, and loading them onto railroad trucks bound for deepest Siberia. The staff constructed false brick walls behind which some statues were hidden, and others were buried almost nine feet underground. (Somehow it was determined that the Germans wouldn't dig deeper than six feet, which proved correct.) For two and half years during the war, the Germans occupied Pavlovsk, looting and ransacking, and when they left in January 1944, they set it ablaze. By the time Soviet troops arrived, it had been burning for three days.

That the people of St. Petersburg resolved immediately to rebuild the palace during a time of enormous suffering was remarkable. In her book *Pavlovsk: The Life of a Russian Palace*, historian Suzanne Massie notes that many people she interviewed about the restoration quoted a line from Dostoevsky, "Beauty will save the world," as explanation for their extraordinary efforts. This sentiment seems integral to the Russian imagination, and restoring the palace to its former glory was a superhuman achievement accomplished against formidable odds. Only original plans and techniques were permitted, and one rather magical result of the restoration process was the creation of a special arts and craft school to teach all-but-lost eighteenth-century techniques, such as gilding, plaster work, and scagliola. Today, in addition to the glorious resurrection of Pavlovsk, there are master craftspeople carrying this legacy forward in Russia and beyond.

Clockwise from top left: A pavilion in the garden at Pavlovsk; Maria Feodorovna's state bedchamber in the palace; the Rose Pavilion in Pavlovsk Park; the palace's picture gallery.

37

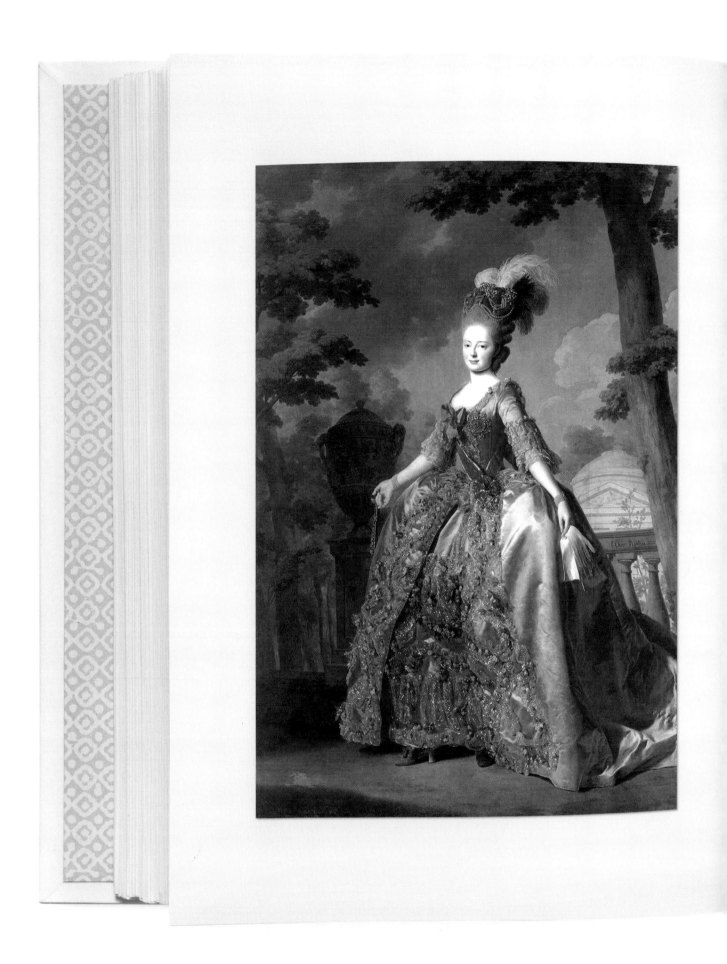

From left to right: *Grand Duchess Maria Feodorovna*, Alexander Roslin, c. 1777. Oil on canvas.
Courtesy of the Hermitage; Tula table in Maria Feodorovna's dressing room at Pavlovsk.

ПП II
84

DINNER AT PAVLOVSK PALACE

FIRST COURSE
Tomato à la Russe

MAIN COURSE
Poulet au Gros Sel

DESSERT
Frozen Lemon Soufflé
with Candied Orange Rind

To create a warm, opulent atmosphere redolent of an elegant winter evening spent in the Rose
Pavilion, Deeda lit the room by candle and incorporated an abundance of roses with a tablecloth
covered in lavish bouquets and an extravagant centerpiece. Photo by Ngoc Minh Ngo.

It would be wonderful to have a dinner anywhere in Pavlovsk, but I did experience a dinner one time in the Rose Pavilion. It is a grand space in the park with a vaulted ceiling covered in bowers of painted roses and an exterior embraced by living ones. Maria Feodorovna loved it as a place to listen to poetry and music amongst artists, writers, and scientists—science was a great stimulus for Russian culture in her day. In keeping with the rose theme of the pavilion, I used a Bennison linen tablecloth covered in large bouquets of soft-hued roses. I asked my friend Cathy Graham to create a lush, almost extravagant, arrangement of old roses, also in soft, slightly dusky tones, to which she added lilacs and hellebore.

For the menu, the first course is a caviar dish, but one I thought Russians might not be familiar with. For each guest, you take a medium-thick slice from a fresh ripe tomato, sprinkle it with a tiny bit of sugar and a small squeeze of lemon, and leave it to marinate a bit before serving. One tomato slice then goes onto each plate, covered by a mixture of crème fraîche and chopped spring onion. Then you gently drop watercress leaves so that they fall casually over the tomato and onto the plate, before topping each serving with a generous helping of caviar.

The second course is a favorite recipe of mine and Bill's from Charles Masson, which was created for his restaurant La Grenouille many years ago. This poulet au gros sel is a wonderful roasted chicken dish that is surrounded by cauliflower, haricots verts, and other vegetables. The two sauces Masson used to serve with it—a cream sauce and a great horseradish sauce—we mix together, because it is easier that way.

Dessert is a heavenly frozen lemon soufflé—the same color as the facade of the palace, and smooth and icy like the snow cover of Russian winters.

Tomato à la Russe on page 170.
Poulet au Gros Sel on page 196.
Frozen Lemon Soufflé on page 220.

Frozen lemon soufflé with candied orange rind set on a marble consul next to Carmen Almon's tole sculpture of plum blossoms.

DINNER AT THE PETIT TRIANON

Soon after the Second World War, Mary Lasker began to return twice a year to Paris. She had developed a deep friendship with Gérald Van der Kemp, who later became the director of Versailles. After one of Mary's early visits to see him at the palace, she noticed there were no guidebooks for visitors and so gave Gérald the funds to develop and print them. These publications helped create a new awareness of Versailles, which eventually led to a lengthy and extensive philanthropic campaign to raise money for a magnificent restoration of the interiors and furnishings of the royal rooms.

During the time we spent there in the 1960s, however, the Petit Trianon, the small château Louis XVI gave to Marie Antoinette, had not yet become the focus of restoration (and would not until the 2000s). Mary and I often dined with Gérald and his wife, Florence, and frequently went for long walks in the gardens of the Petit Trianon. Those gardens, almost more than those around the palace, were our favorite to walk in, and we spent more time at the Petit Trianon than in Le Nôtre's legendary landscape. As Gérald had the keys, we would also wander through the unrestored, but hauntingly beautiful, and mostly empty, interior of the château.

Marie Antoinette had asked her husband for a country house as a refuge from court life, and in 1774, when she was nineteen, the king was said to have slipped into her hand a key to the Petit Trianon on a keyring adorned with 531 diamonds. The château became her private residence—much simpler than the palace, and with far less gilding and grandeur. The king, it was said, was permitted to visit by invitation only. Here, Marie Antoinette indulged in her fantasy of pastoral life, often wearing dresses of white muslin with a colored sash around the waist and wide-brimmed straw hats trimmed with feathers and ribbons to tend to her flowers and her menagerie. It was rumored that even the lambs were perfumed.

The extraordinary gardens Marie Antoinette created continue to be brought back to life. The grounds, as originally commissioned by Louis XV, featured elaborate formal floral displays and collections of rare imported botanical plants. When Marie Antoinette arrived, she sent the pineapple and coffee plants off to the palace greenhouses. She had a far more romantic vision: a naturalistic garden, in part influenced by the picturesque English landscapes of the period, with flowering meadows, fields of grazing sheep, and meandering streams. The queen was also responsible for a pair of follies—the Belvedere Pavilion and the Temple of Love—two of the most wonderful buildings you could ever imagine, which remain important examples of neoclassical garden architecture.

Previous spread: An intimate dinner for two, inspired by Marie Antoinette's private quarters, is set in front of the fireplace in the living room, with a loose bouquet to invoke her garden, which was more wild and natural in style than the formal gardens of Versailles.

Today, the interior of the Petit Trianon is exquisite. The first floors are arranged around the staircase, and rooms open directly onto the gardens. When it was restored, some of the original furniture commissioned by Marie Antoinette was brought back. There is a ravishing set of beautifully carved and painted furniture in her bedroom, called "wheat ear" furniture, made by Georges Jacob, one of the most skilled furniture makers of the period. It is said to be the most expensive furniture ever made. And yet, in contrast to the palace, the decoration could almost be called simple; there were muslins instead of silks, and the paint on the walls and the furniture was in the colors of a garden in springtime—pale blues, greens, and pinks—instead of gold.

All of Marie Antoinette's work at the Petit Trianon was done at immense expense, which some say contributed to the revolution. Yet, today it stands as her legacy to the public.

Clockwise from top left: *View of the Temple*, Richard Mique, 1786. Ink and watercolor on paper. 13¾ x 18½ in. (34.9 x 47 cm); Marie Antoinette's bedroom at the Petit Trianon; Louis XVI–style armchair and footstool by Georges Jacob in the queen's sitting room at Petit Trianon; the Belvedere Pavilion at Versailles.

THE PETIT TRIANON

From left to right: *Marie Antoinette in a Muslin Dress*, Élisabeth Vigée Le Brun, 1783. Oil on canvas. 35⅜ x 28⅜ in. (89.8 x 72 cm); some of Deeda's favorite roses.

THE PETIT TRIANON

DINNER AT THE PETIT TRIANON

FIRST COURSE
Caviar Soufflé

MAIN COURSE

Lobster Tiede Surrounded
with Clusters of Baby Vegetables
with Beurre Blanc

DESSERT
Vesuvius Ice Cream Mold
with Chocolate Lace

This caviar soufflé, with its scattering of microgreens spilling onto the plate, reflects the sense of simplicity, achieved with great extravagance, of Marie Antoinette's pastoral refuge on the grounds of Versailles. Photo by Ngoc Minh Ngo.

Lobster Tiede surrounded with Clusters of Baby Vegetables

When I began working on the menu for the Petit Trianon meal, my first thoughts were of the huge court menus served at Versailles, frequently consisting of at least twenty-four courses! I suspected this would not be of great interest to Marie Antoinette with her fiercely tight-waisted dresses, nor is it to me.

Three courses are sufficient, but I felt the menu should have a sense of fantasy. I have never had this caviar soufflé recipe in anyone else's home, and while it looks spectacular and indulgent, we use relatively reasonably priced paddlefish caviar from Tennessee. What is needed is to be able to put it together with speed. I like to serve it in individual soufflé dishes rather than one big platter of food that you are cutting into and messing up. For that reason, I experimented, and finally came up with these individual caviar soufflés, to which we add crème fraîche with minced scallion. We also put a handful of microgreens on the soufflé and let some of the leaves flutter onto the plate. It is not difficult, but it does look special.

The second course of lobster is rather special and attractive.

The Vesuvius ice cream is one of my absolute favorite desserts—it looks spectacular, and people always take seconds. Guests are surprised when it first comes out, and then again when they cut into it and the finely ground dark chocolate spills out. At court, they had so many chefs and enormous, elaborately decorated, fantastical things, so I did want this dessert to look extravagant but to also be simple. It has become difficult to find the molds nowadays—you can make this dish in a Bundt pan, though it won't have the same wonderful swirl on the top. If you can't find the chocolate lace, which we buy at Grace's Marketplace in my neighborhood, it can be served with fudge sauce instead.

For this meal, I used my prettiest silk tablecloth, which I had hand-painted by Gracie & Company. I found the trim for it in Manhattan's flower district. We set a table for two in front of the fireplace in the living room, and the plates are eighteenth-century Sèvres I have collected, dating from Marie Antoinette's time. With the flowers, I wanted to evoke the romance of her garden, so I aimed for them to feel a little bit wild, rather than being too restrained and formal. We used a mix of vines and roses arranged very loosely, so it almost feels as if they're growing.

Caviar Soufflé on page 173.
Lobster Tiede Surrounded with Clusters of Baby Vegetables
    with Beurre Blanc on page 204.
Vesuvius Ice Cream Mold with Chocolate Lace on page 231.
Schrafft's Fudge Sauce on page 239.

Following spread: The Vesuvius dessert is made with vanilla ice cream set in a mold, with chocolate bark at its base, and a secret chocolate sauce, or "lava," inside.

PART III

RECIPES

162	Soups
168	First Courses
176	Lunches & Salads
186	Pasta
192	Poultry & Meat
202	Fish & Lobster
208	Vegetables
214	Cakes, Tarts, Soufflés & Cookies
226	Ice Cream, Sorbets & Fruit Desserts
234	Sauces & Special Favorites

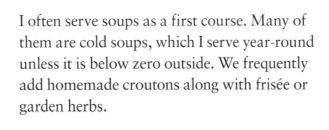

SOUPS

I often serve soups as a first course. Many of them are cold soups, which I serve year-round unless it is below zero outside. We frequently add homemade croutons along with frisée or garden herbs.

164   Deeda's Iced Cauliflower Soup with Crisp Croutons
166   Delicate Vegetable Soup
       Cold Pea, Potato, and Lettuce Soup
167   Deeda's Cold Beet Soup
       Crème Aurore

Deeda's Iced Cauliflower Soup with Crisp Croutons

1 large head cauliflower
1 medium yellow onion, thinly sliced
1 small rib celery, thinly sliced
3 cups chicken stock
Salt to taste
Cayenne pepper or crushed red pepper
    to taste
¼ cup cream or half and half
1 tablespoon minced chives
¼ cup crushed ice
Shredded frisée and croutons for garnish

Note
To crush the ice for this soup, I put ice
cubes in an old dish towel and strike the
bundle with a hammer!

Chop the cauliflower roughly. Take 1 cup of the chopped cauliflower and chop it more finely into pieces the size of peas. Set aside.

Place the onion and celery in a large saucepan with water just to cover; season and simmer until soft.

Meanwhile, place the roughly chopped cauliflower in a pot with a generous amount of cold water. Bring to a boil, simmer for 5 to 6 minutes, until softened but still firm in the center, and drain.

Add the blanched cauliflower to the saucepan with the onion and celery. Add the stock, season with salt and hot pepper, and cook until the cauliflower is just tender.

Puree with a blender or food processor. Stir in the cream and the chives. Refrigerate until very cold.

Divide the soup among four individual bowls. Stir about ⅓ cup of the finely chopped reserved cauliflower into each portion. Stir 1 tablespoon of crushed ice into each portion, then garnish with frisée and croutons and serve immediately before the ice melts.

Serves 4

Delicate Vegetable Soup

This is a variation on a deliciously creamy soup I learned from a long-gone teacher in Paris from whom I took a short course years ago.

4 to 5 leeks
5 tablespoons unsalted butter
1 pound (about 5 medium) potatoes, peeled
      and quartered
5 ounces (about 1 cup) frozen peas, thawed
2 egg yolks
½ cup sour cream
About 1 ½ cups milk
Salt and freshly ground black pepper to taste

Note
It can be served either hot or cold.
If I'm serving it hot, I like to top it with
fried croutons; if it's cold, I sprinkle on
some shredded lettuce.

Slice the leeks lengthwise and in a stockpot or Dutch oven sweat them in 3 tablespoons of the butter for 10 minutes without browning. Add the potatoes and 2 cups water and bring to the boil. Cover and simmer until the potatoes are soft, 40 to 45 minutes. Add the peas and cook to heat them through, then put the mixture through a food mill.

Combine the egg yolks, sour cream, and the remaining 2 tablespoons of butter in a small bowl. Return the mixture that has gone through the food mill to the pot and add 1 ½ cups milk. Bring to a boil while stirring constantly. When the soup begins to bubble, ladle about ¼ cup of it into the bowl with the egg yolk mixture and whisk briskly to combine, then add the yolk mixture to the pot with the soup and cook, still stirring constantly, until heated through. If the soup is too thick for your liking, thin it with a little more milk. Season to taste.

Serve hot or cold.

Serves 4

Cold Pea, Potato, and Lettuce Soup

10 ounces (about 2 cups) frozen peas,
      partially thawed, or 1 ½ cups shelled
      fresh peas
1 medium potato, peeled and diced
1 medium yellow onion, chopped
1 head Boston lettuce, cored and quartered
2 cups chicken broth or stock
1 cup heavy cream
Juice of ½ lemon
Salt and freshly ground black pepper to taste
Shredded lettuce for garnish
Celery salt to taste (optional)

Note
This is terrific cold or hot, and the color is
a lovely pale green. This can also be served
with croutons.

Put peas, potato, onion, Boston lettuce quarters, and 1 cup of the chicken broth in a saucepan. Bring just to a boil. Lower heat, cover, and simmer for 10 minutes.

Puree smooth in a blender. Return the soup to the saucepan, add the remaining 1 cup of broth, and simmer for 5 minutes. Add the cream and lemon juice, and season to taste with salt and pepper. Chill.

To serve, garnish with finely shredded crisp lettuce with a dusting of celery salt if you desire.

Serves 4

Deeda's Cold Beet Soup

This is a favorite soup that has been in my family for fifty years. It is a very beautiful color and looks wonderful served in a small glass bowl.

1 bunch (4 to 5 medium) beets
1 small yellow onion, chopped
2 cups chicken consommé
Salt and freshly ground black pepper to taste
Sugar to taste
About 1 tablespoon freshly squeezed
    lemon juice
⅓ cup light cream
Chopped chives and edible flowers
    for garnish

Note
You can also steam an extra beet, chop it coarsely, and use it as a garnish in place of the chives and flowers.

Peel and thinly slice the beets. Simmer the beets and the onion in the consommé for 30 minutes. Allow the mixture to cool.

Cool and put the above mixture into a blender to puree bas smooth as you like; I serve it slightly chunky. Season to taste with salt, pepper, sugar, and lemon juice. Chill for several hours before serving. (The soup can also be frozen at this stage.)

Just before serving, dilute the soup with the cream. Stir well, distribute among individual serving bowls, and garnish.

Serves 4

Crème Aurore

This cream of tomato and potato is another soup adapted from a French cooking school course that I've been making for many years.

3 tablespoons unsalted butter
6 potatoes, peeled and thinly sliced
1 yellow onion, thinly sliced
3 leeks, thinly sliced
2 cloves garlic, thinly sliced
Salt and freshly ground black pepper to taste
2 cups whole milk
1 pound ripe tomatoes, sliced, or
    1 28-ounce can Campari tomatoes
½ teaspoon tomato paste
¼ cup light cream
Homemade tiny croutons for garnish

Melt 2 tablespoons of the butter in a Dutch oven and add the potatoes, half of the onion, the leeks, and the garlic with ½ cup water. Season and cook over low heat, stirring occasionally, until soft. Combine the milk with 1 cup water, add to the vegetables, and bring to a boil. Remove from the heat.

Melt the remaining 1 tablespoon butter in a skillet and add the remaining sliced onion. Cook over medium-high heat, stirring frequently, until it begins to color, 2 to 3 minutes. Add the tomatoes and tomato paste and season with salt and pepper. Cook over low heat, stirring frequently, for 5 minutes. Force the tomato mixture through a strainer and add to the soup. (You can force it through the strainer directly into the pot.) Bring the mixture back to a boil, stirring frequently, and stir in the cream. Continue to cook, stirring, until heated through, then garnish with croutons and serve.

Serves 4

FIRST COURSES

I usually serve three courses, whether for lunch or dinner. If I'm not serving a soup, I serve other dishes, from caviar to pasta to salad, in small portions as starters. I always serve individual portions, rather than dishing the food out from a large platter at the table, because they look so attractive plated and when guests walk into the room there is already something on the table.

170	Tomato à la Russe
172	Deeda's Lychee Salad
	Truffled Tagliolini
173	Cold Vegetables with Herbs and Vinaigrette
	Caviar Soufflés
174	Homemade Potato Chips with Crème Fraîche and Caviar

Tomato à la Russe

Caviar needn't break the bank. I use American paddlefish roe, which is very reasonably priced and pleasantly mild, rather than imported caviar. It comes via FedEx packed in ice. See page 244 for source.

1 slice sandwich bread

1 tablespoon unsalted butter

1 ¾-inch-thick slice of peeled tomato

1 pinch sugar

A few drops of freshly squeezed lemon juice

2 tablespoons crème fraîche

1 teaspoon minced spring onion

2 to 3 tablespoons caviar

½ cup lightly packed watercress leaves and sprigs (any thick stems removed)

1 teaspoon Favorite Vinaigrette (page 237)

With a round cookie cutter, cut a circle out of the slice of bread that is the same diameter as the tomato slice you are using. Melt the butter in a skillet and toast the circle of bread on both sides until just golden.

Place the crouton on a plate. Top with the tomato slice. Sprinkle the tomato with the sugar and lemon juice. In a small bowl mix the crème fraîche with the spring onion. Spread the mixture on top of the tomato and top with enough caviar to cover the surface of the crème fraîche generously, leaving a small border around the perimeter. Toss the watercress with the vinaigrette and arrange it around the tomato. Serve immediately.

Serves 1

FIRST COURSES

Deeda's Lychee Salad

Salad
½ cup cream cheese, very cold
2 teaspoons celery salt
3 ripe avocados, halved and pitted
2 tablespoons fresh lemon juice
1 cup peeled and seeded fresh lychees
2 navel oranges, peeled and sliced into
⅛ inch-thick rounds
2 scallions (white parts only), thinly
sliced diagonally
8 cups romaine lettuce torn into bite-
sized pieces
¼ cup finely chopped watercress leaves

Dressing
1 teaspoon paprika
½ teaspoon dry mustard powder
1 teaspoon salt
1 teaspoon Worcestershire sauce
1 teaspoon minced garlic
½ cup red wine vinegar
2 cups neutral vegetable oil
1 heaping cup finely chopped watercress
leaves

Note
Fresh lychees are delicious, but if they are
unavailable, the kind canned in water (or
syrup) will work as well. Rinse and drain
them thoroughly.

With a small melon baller, scoop balls the size of a marble from the cream cheese. Roll the balls in the celery salt and refrigerate. With the same small melon baller, make 1 cup of balls from the avocados. Toss with the lemon juice and refrigerate.

In a large salad bowl, toss together the lychees, orange slices, scallions, romaine lettuce, and watercress leaves. Set aside.

To make the dressing, in a medium bowl, combine the paprika, dry mustard, salt, Worcestershire sauce, and garlic. Add the vinegar and oil and whisk until the dressing is thoroughly combined. Add the very generous cup of finely chopped watercress. (It is not possible to have too much watercress.)

Add the avocado balls and ¾ cup of the dressing to the salad and very gently toss. Taste for seasoning and add more dressing if desired. Sprinkle the cream cheese balls on top and serve.

Serves 4 to 6

Truffled Tagliolini

This is a simple recipe, but extravagant and wonderful.

6 ounces tagliolini, broken in half
6 tablespoons unsalted butter, at room
temperature
¼ cup crème fraîche, at room temperature
About 1 teaspoon truffle salt
Grated fresh truffle to taste

Note
For tagliolini, I like the Cipriani brand.

Prepare tagliolini the Italian way: cook in lots of (unsalted) boiling water, being careful not to overcook.

When the tagliolini is cooked, drain it in a colander and transfer it to a saucepan with the butter. Toss over low heat, taking care not to let the butter brown, but only melt. Remove from the heat, add the crème fraîche, and toss to combine. Salt generously with truffle salt, which enhances the taste of the fresh truffle. Grate the fresh truffle on top and serve immediately.

Serves 4

Cold Vegetables with Herbs and Vinaigrette

New potatoes, blanched, chilled, and
tossed with chopped flat-leaf parsley
Baby carrots, blanched, chilled, and
tossed with chopped dill
Cauliflower florets, blanched and chilled
Broccoli florets, blanched, chilled, and
tossed with chopped tarragon
Avocado, peeled, pitted, and sliced
Mushrooms, sliced
Cherry tomatoes
Cucumbers, seeded, sliced, and tossed
with Homemade Mayonnaise
(page 236)
Asparagus sprinkled with chopped
hard-boiled egg
Favorite Vinaigrette (page 237)
Chopped watercress
Freshly squeezed lemon juice

Note
This recipe works well with any of the
vegetables mentioned. This is based on
classic French crudités, but some of the
vegetables are blanched. The proportions
are up to you.

Arrange the vegetables (except for the watercress) on plates.
It is important to make an attractive combination of colors.

Combine the vinaigrette with the watercress and lemon juice and
drizzle it over the vegetables to coat lightly.

Caviar Soufflés

Butter for ramekins
¾ cup sour cream or crème fraîche
3 tablespoons minced scallions
6 eggs, separated
Cayenne pepper to taste
Seasoned salt to taste
Salt and freshly ground black pepper to taste
½ cup microgreens, well-dried
¾ cup caviar

Note
The ramekins for these individual soufflés
are 3 ¼ inches in diameter and 2 inches
high, or 5-ounce round ramekins. They are
available at Sur la Table and other kitchenware stores.

Preheat the oven to 475°F. Butter six 5-ounce ramekins and set aside.
Combine the sour cream and scallions and set aside.

In a large bowl, beat the egg yolks and then season with the cayenne,
both types of salt, and black pepper. Set aside.

In a large bowl, beat the egg whites until stiff. Gently fold the egg
whites into the yolk mixture. Divide the egg mixture between the
buttered ramekins. Bake the soufflés until risen, about 5 minutes.

Remove the soufflés from the oven and, working quickly, top each
with microgreens, 2 tablespoons sour cream mixture, and 2 tablespoons caviar, in that order. Serve immediately. Speed is essential!

Makes 6 individual soufflés

Homemade Potato Chips with Crème Fraîche and Caviar

This is very simple, but everybody adores it.

2 medium waxy potatoes
1 stick (8 tablespoons) unsalted butter,
    melted
Salt to taste
1 cup crème fraîche
½ cup unsweetened whipped cream
2 tablespoons minced scallions
1 ½ cups caviar

Preheat oven to 500°F.

Peel the potatoes and slice crosswise ¹⁄₁₆-inch thick on a mandoline. Rinse the slices in several changes of cold water until the water runs clear. Pat very dry with paper towels.

Dip the potatoes in the butter and arrange them in a single layer on baking sheets. Put the pans on separate racks in the oven and bake for 10 minutes. Reverse the position of the pans top to bottom and front to back and bake until crisp and browned, about 10 additional minutes. Remove from the oven and lightly salt. Push the chips off the sheets with a pancake turner. Put a towel over them if they have to wait.

Fold together the crème fraîche, whipped cream, and scallions. On each of four salad plates, place a generous group of overlapping chips. Dollop 6 generous spoonfuls of the crème fraîche mixture on each plate. Place a generous spoonful of caviar on top of each dollop of crème fraîche mixture, and serve.

Serves 4

Anonymous, *Beta vulgaris*, 1 plate, v. *Beta*, 16, plate 9.

LUNCHES & SALADS

These are main dishes that I usually serve at luncheons. Most have chicken or lobster but can easily be prepared without. I love to serve soufflés at lunch, which I generally try to keep fairly light.

178	Gruyère Roulade
180	Pea Salad with Shredded Chicken
	Chopped Salad
181	Henry McIlhenny's Cold Tomato Soufflé
182	Coronation Chicken Salad
184	Moroccan Chicken and Couscous
	Lobster and Grapefruit Salad
185	Pasta Soufflé

Gruyère Roulade

This is essentially a soufflé wrapped in a roll around a salad! A friend gave me this recipe almost forty years ago because she knew I would love it, and indeed it has become a great favorite.

Roulade
½ cup grated Parmigiano Reggiano
12 ounces Gruyère cheese, grated
1 cup fresh white breadcrumbs
8 eggs, separated
1 ¼ cups light cream
Salt to taste
1 teaspoon cayenne pepper
2 tablespoons hot water

Filling
¼ cup plus 1 tablespoon Homemade
    Mayonnaise (page 236)
¼ cup sour cream
4 scallions, finely chopped
24 cherry tomatoes, halved
½ cup 1-inch slices steamed haricots verts
½ cup sliced radishes or sliced
    raw mushrooms
2 cooked artichoke bottoms cut into julienne
2 large leaves Romaine lettuce, finely
    shredded
1 cup watercress leaves
2 avocados, peeled, seeded, and thinly
    sliced (optional)
½ cup halved steamed baby brussels
    sprouts (optional)
½ cup thinly sliced steamed broccoli,
    asparagus, or baby zucchini (optional)
Salt and freshly ground black pepper to taste

Note
For a smaller roulade, cut the quantities in half and use a 9 by 13-inch jellyroll pan.

Heat the oven to 400°F. Line a 15 ½ by 10 ½-inch jellyroll pan with parchment paper and sprinkle with some of the grated Parmigiano to coat lightly.

Combine the Gruyère, breadcrumbs, egg yolks, and cream in a bowl. Season with salt and cayenne. Stir in the hot water.

Add a pinch of salt to the egg whites and beat until they form soft peaks. Fold the egg whites into the cheese mixture and spread it evenly in the prepared pan.

Bake in center of oven until risen and firm to a light touch, 20 to 25 minutes. Remove and cover with a damp cloth to prevent it from drying out as it comes to room temperature.

Sprinkle a sheet of parchment paper with more Parmigiano. Flip the roulade onto this new sheet of parchment and peel off the parchment that was underneath while it baked. Combine the mayonnaise and sour cream and spread it on the surface. Sprinkle on the scallions, then tomatoes, haricots verts, radishes, artichokes, and finally lettuce, watercress, and any optional vegetables. Season with salt and pepper.

Roll up fairly loosely with the help of the parchment paper and transfer carefully to a serving dish. Don't worry if it splits. This just proves how light it is. Also, don't try to roll it up too tightly, or the filling will squeeze out!

Just before serving sprinkle with the remaining Parmigiano.

Serves 6 to 8

Pea Salad with Shredded Chicken

Salad
4 medium beets
1 tablespoon extra-virgin olive oil
3 tablespoons neutral vegetable oil
Salt to taste
1 head cauliflower, chopped into florets
1 ⅓ cups frozen peas, thawed
2 to 3 cups mesclun
4 to 6 Romaine lettuce leaves, torn
16 cherry tomatoes, halved
2 cups shredded cooked chicken

Dressing and Sauce
Juice of 1 lemon
2 tablespoons neutral vegetable oil
1 teaspoon minced garlic
Wasabi to taste
2 tablespoons low-fat Greek yogurt
2 tablespoons creamed horseradish
Freshly ground black pepper

Note
A composed salad is a great way to use up leftover roasted chicken. You can also poach chicken breasts and use them here.

Preheat the oven to 350°F.

Coat the beets with the two types of oil and wrap them tightly in aluminum foil. Place the packet in a baking pan and roast until the beets are tender, 45 to 50 minutes. Let the beets cool, then peel them (the peels should slip right off) and cut them into bite-sized pieces.

Prepare a bowl of ice water. Bring a pot of water to a boil, salt it lightly, and blanch the cauliflower in a pan of boiling salted water for 1 minute, then add about half of the peas and cook for 1 additional minute. Drain the vegetables, then shock them in the ice water. Drain them again.

In a bowl combine the beets, cauliflower, cooked peas, mesclun, Romaine, tomatoes, and chicken.

For the dressing, whisk together the lemon juice, vegetable oil, garlic, and wasabi and drizzle it over the salad. Toss to combine. Arrange the salad on each plate in a tall mound and sprinkle the remaining peas on top so they cascade down the side. In a small bowl, combine the yogurt and horseradish and spoon it on top of the salad. Season with black pepper.

Serves 4

Chopped Salad

This is a variation on a salad that used to be served poolside at the Beverly Hills Hotel in California.

1 cup of julienne strips of Swiss cheese
2 cups finely shredded romaine lettuce
1 ½ cups peeled, seeded, and chopped
    fresh tomatoes
¾ cup chopped avocado
1 cup shredded cooked chicken breast
4 hard-boiled eggs, peeled and finely
    chopped
4 cooked beets, peeled and chopped into
    pieces slightly larger than the size
    of a pea
½ cup Homemade Mayonnaise (page 236)
¼ cup unsweetened whipped cream
1 teaspoon ketchup
2 cloves garlic, crushed with a garlic press
    or minced
Cayenne pepper to taste
6 pieces bacon, fried crisp

For the salad, mix the cheese, lettuce, tomatoes, avocado, and chicken breast. Stir in most of the hard-boiled egg, reserving about ¼ cup for garnish. Add the beets and toss gently. In a small bowl, mix the mayonnaise, whipped cream, ketchup, and garlic. Add cayenne pepper to taste, just a sprinkling.

Toss the salad with the dressing to combine well. Place a ring mold on one of four individual plates. Arrange about ¼ of the salad in the ring mold and gently remove the mold. Repeat with remaining servings. Sprinkle remaining hard-boiled egg and then the chopped bacon on top and serve.

Serves 4

Henry McIlhenny's Cold Tomato Soufflé

Henry was a great Philadelphia art collector and curator, and this recipe is adapted from a dish he served. It is really only good in summer, when one has delicious fresh tomatoes, rather than the hothouse ones.

2 ½ pounds (8 to 9) ripe tomatoes
¾ cup Homemade Mayonnaise (page 236)
2 to 3 envelopes unflavored gelatin powder
2 tablespoons tomato paste
2 teaspoons lemon juice
1 teaspoon salt, plus more to taste
2 teaspoons sugar, plus more to taste
¾ cup whipping cream
¼ cup Favorite Vinaigrette (page 237)
Chopped basil to garnish

Cut an X in the bottom of each of 5 tomatoes. Bring a pot of water to a boil, blanch the tomatoes in boiling water for 1 minute, then remove with a slotted spoon and peel. Cut the tomatoes horizontally and squeeze to remove seeds. Cut out and discard any whitish cores. Cut the peeled tomatoes into 1-inch chunks. In a blender, puree the peeled tomatoes with the mayonnaise until smooth. Measure the volume of the tomato puree. You will need 1 envelope of gelatin for every 2 cups of the mixture.

Let the gelatin bloom in a few tablespoons of cold water, then combine thoroughly with the tomato puree. Add the tomato paste, lemon juice, 1 teaspoon salt, and 2 teaspoons sugar to the tomato puree and taste to adjust seasoning. Note that this soufflé will be served cold, thus the taste will be diminished. Chill the mixture until it is set.

Whip the cream until soft peaks form. Whip the chilled tomato mixture until it is fluffy and soft, but not melted. Fold in the whipped cream until the white streaks disappear.

Create a parchment collar around the perimeter of a 7- to 8-inch round soufflé dish. Wrap a glass jar (approximately 2 ½ inches in diameter and 5 inches high) in plastic wrap and place it in the center of the soufflé dish. Fill the jar with water to steady it. Pour the chilled tomato mixture into the soufflé dish around the upright jar. Chill the soufflé until firm.

Carefully remove the jar from the soufflé dish. Chop the remaining tomatoes into ¾-inch pieces and toss them with the vinaigrette. Fill the central cavity with the dressed tomatoes and garnish with the basil.

Serves 4

Coronation Chicken Salad

This is adapted from the chicken dish that Rory Cameron would serve at La Fiorentina, which in turn was based on a recipe originally created by Constance Spry for Queen Elizabeth II's coronation lunch.

¼ cup plus 2 tablespoons Homemade Mayonnaise (page 236)
1 tablespoon apricot preserves (heated and passed through a sieve)
2 teaspoons curry powder
¼ cup plus 2 tablespoons unsweetened whipped cream
2 to 3 chicken breasts, poached, cooled, and pulled into long strips
1 cup halved green grapes
Bibb or Boston lettuce leaves and frisée, for serving
2 ripe avocadoes
Juice of 1 lemon
Salt and freshly ground black pepper to taste
½ cup toasted sliced almonds
1 cup mango chutney
2 green bananas, thinly sliced

Just before serving, fold together the mayonnaise, preserves, curry powder, and whipped cream. In a large bowl toss the chicken and grapes, then dress with the mayonnaise mixture and toss to combine.

On each serving plate, make a fan of overlapping lettuce leaves. Peel, pit, and slice the avocados and toss the slices with the lemon juice, then place a few slices of avocado on top of each serving of lettuce. Season with salt and pepper. Next to the lettuce, arrange a serving of the chicken mixture.

Place the almonds, chutney, and green bananas in separate lacquer or glass bowls and pass them on the side to allow guests to finish their own salads as they desire. A little chopped crisp bacon is also delicious.

Serves 4 to 6

Moroccan Chicken and Couscous

This is one of my most frequently requested recipes.

3 cups chicken broth

1 ½ cups couscous

1 tablespoon chopped flat-leaf parsley

2 tablespoons freshly squeezed lemon juice

3 tablespoons extra-virgin olive oil

3 teaspoons hot curry powder

¼ teaspoon freshly ground black pepper

1 teaspoon crushed red pepper

6 ounces snow peas, blanched and cut into
    julienne (about 2 cups)

1 ½ cups shredded cooked chicken breast

1 teaspoon minced garlic

¾ cup thinly sliced scallion

½ cup golden raisins plumped in white wine

½ cup shredded carrot

8 dried apricots plumped in white wine,
    drained, and cut into julienne

2 cups halved green grapes

½ cup coarsely chopped toasted pecans

Bring the chicken broth to a boil in a medium saucepan. Stir in the couscous and parsley. Remove the pan from heat, cover, and let stand 5 minutes until broth is absorbed.

Meanwhile in a large bowl whisk the lemon juice, oil, curry powder, black pepper, and crushed red pepper. Add the cooked couscous and toss to coat. Add the snow peas, chicken, garlic, scallion, raisins, carrot, dried apricots, and grapes. Toss to mix well.

Cover and refrigerate for at least 30 minutes. Just before serving, give the mixture a good stir. Divide among four plates and sprinkle each portion with pecans.

Serves 4

Lobster and Grapefruit Salad

I love salads with citrus fruits like this one.

2 lobsters, cooked

1 orange

2 grapefruits

1 avocado

1 teaspoon lemon juice

1 teaspoon vegetable oil

2 teaspoons extra-virgin olive oil

½ teaspoon minced garlic

1 teaspoon minced chervil

1 teaspoon minced tarragon

1 heaping teaspoon Dijon mustard

Salt and freshly ground black pepper to taste

Crushed red pepper or cayenne pepper
    to taste (optional)

Leaves of 1 small head bibb lettuce

1 cup torn frisée

Shell the lobsters, extract the meat, slice it, and set it aside. Peel the orange and the grapefruits and cut them into supremes, removing and discarding any white pith and the membranes between the sections. Peel, pit, and slice the avocado. Combine the citrus and avocado in a large bowl.

Combine the lemon juice, vegetable oil, olive oil, garlic, chervil, and tarragon. Whisk to combine, then whisk in the mustard. Season with salt and pepper and the crushed red pepper, if using. Add the lobster to the citrus and avocado, and toss the lobster salad with the dressing.

Combine the lettuce leaves and frisée and use them to make beds on two individual plates. Arrange a portion of the salad on each and serve immediately.

Serves 2

Pasta Soufflé

Soufflés can be daunting if you haven't made one, but once you've made one successfully, you'll feel so triumphant and you'll want to do more.

4 tablespoons unsalted butter, plus more
    for buttering dish
1 cup heavy cream
1 ½ cups béchamel (recipe below)
6 ounces tagliolini or angel hair
1 cup freshly grated Parmigiano Reggiano
6 large eggs, separated
1 teaspoon freshly ground black pepper
1 teaspoon cayenne pepper
1 teaspoon salt or truffle salt
1 egg white

Note
I like Cipriani brand tagliolini, but angel hair pasta will also work.

Preheat the oven to 375°F. Butter an 8-cup soufflé dish (7 ½ inches in diameter and 3 ½ inches high).

Add the heavy cream to the béchamel sauce and cook over low heat for 1 to 2 minutes to warm through. Remove from heat.

Bring a large pot of water to a boil and salt it. Cook the pasta in the boiling water until just al dente. Drain. You should have 1 ½ cups of cooked pasta. Add the pasta, Parmigiano, and 4 tablespoons butter to the béchamel mixture and stir to combine. Lightly beat the 6 egg yolks and stir them into the mixture. Season with pepper, cayenne, and salt.

Beat the 7 egg whites until they form stiff peaks but are not dry. Fold about one-quarter of the egg whites into the pasta mixture. Don't rush and fold them in using a half-circle gesture, as you are trying to get as much air as possible into the mixture. When the first addition is incorporated, gently fold in the rest.

Pour the mixture into the prepared soufflé dish. Bake until puffed and browned, 40 to 45 minutes. Serve immediately.

Serves 6

Béchamel Sauce
Makes about 1 ½ cups

1 ½ cups whole milk
3 tablespoons unsalted butter
¼ cup all-purpose flour
¼ teaspoon salt

Bring the milk to a boil in a small saucepan over medium heat. Meanwhile, melt the butter in a small heavy saucepan over low heat. Whisk the flour into the butter with a wire whisk and cook, stirring constantly, until incorporated but not browned, 1 to 2 minutes. Remove from the heat.

Add the warm milk all at once, stirring vigorously with the whisk to prevent lumps from forming. Add salt and stir. Return the pan to the burner and cook the sauce for a few minutes longer, stirring constantly, until it is about the thickness of sour cream.

186

PASTA

I serve these dishes as main courses for both
lunches and dinners, but more frequently
at lunch. I like to use thin, delicate pastas that
highlight the fresh ingredients of the sauces,
allowing their flavors to remain distinct.
In this way, the dishes feel light rather than
starchy or too filling.

188   Cold Spaghetti Salad
        Fresh Zucchini "Pasta"
189   Le Cirque's Pasta Primavera
190   Ina Garten's Spinach and Ricotta Lasagna
191   Deeda's Green Pasta with Vegetables and Bacon
        Chicken Pasta with Fried Croutons

Cold Spaghetti Salad

This recipe dates back to the late 1960s or early 1970s and was given to me by Donina Cicogna, a sparkling Italian woman who had a lively charm that was quite magical. I believe this may be the first cold pasta salad; it was certainly the first and the best I've ever had. She served it as a first course at a long lunch in the south of France, and I wished I could just go on eating it.

Juice of ½ lemon
½ cup extra-virgin olive oil
1 clove garlic, minced
1 tablespoon Dijon mustard
Cayenne pepper to taste
Wasabi to taste
1 cup cooked long thin pasta, such as spaghetti, angel hair, or tagliolini, cut into thirds and cooled
6 cups peeled tomatoes sliced into ½-inch-thick strips 1 to 2 inches long or cherry tomatoes (or more—you almost can't have too many tomatoes in this dish)
½ cup very thin strips ham
½ cup thinly sliced celery
1 cup shredded iceberg lettuce
½ cup thinly sliced radishes
2 teaspoons capers
2 cups fresh basil

Combine the lemon juice, olive oil, garlic, mustard, cayenne, and wasabi, and whisk to combine.

In a large bowl combine the pasta, 5 cups of the tomatoes, ham, celery, lettuce, radishes, capers, and 1 cup basil. Toss with the vinaigrette. Scatter the remaining 1 cup tomatoes and 1 cup basil on top, and serve at room temperature.

Serves 2

Fresh Zucchini "Pasta"

This is awfully good and very healthy, as the "pasta" is actually fresh zucchini cut long and thin to resemble spaghetti.

½ cup finely chopped cauliflower
½ cup finely chopped broccoli
2 tablespoons unsalted butter
½ yellow onion, chopped
1 clove garlic, minced
2 medium zucchini, about 8 ounces, cut into spaghetti with a spiralizer
2 large tomatoes, cut into small dice
½ cup crème fraîche
Salt and freshly ground black pepper to taste
½ cup torn basil leaves

Steam the cauliflower and broccoli until tender. In a large skillet, melt the butter. Add the onion and garlic and cook until they begin to color, then add the zucchini noodles and cook until softened, 3 to 4 minutes. Add the cauliflower and broccoli and toss to combine. Add the tomatoes and cook for 2 additional minutes. Stir in the crème fraîche and season with salt and pepper. Scatter the basil on top and serve.

Serves 4

Le Cirque's Pasta Primavera

While pasta primavera has fallen out of fashion somewhat since Sirio Maccioni of Le Cirque invented it in the 1970s, it is still simple and delicious and works well with whatever vegetables you have on hand.

½ bunch broccoli
½ small head cauliflower
2 small zucchini
2 cups frozen peas
½ cup 1 ½-inch slices haricots verts
8 Campari tomatoes
Sugar to taste
Salt and freshly ground black pepper to taste
1 to 2 teaspoons lemon juice
2 cloves garlic, minced
3 tablespoons extra-virgin olive oil
2 to 3 tablespoons minced flat-leaf parsley
¼ teaspoon crushed red pepper
3 tablespoons torn basil leaves
¼ cup heavy cream
1 tablespoon chicken broth
4 ounces spaghetti or other pasta
2 tablespoons melted butter
⅓ cup grated Parmigiano Reggiano
6 strips bacon, cooked crisp and chopped
¼ cup toasted pine nuts

Chop the broccoli and cauliflower into bite-sized pieces. Trim the zucchini and cut into quarters lengthwise, then cut each quarter into 1-inch lengths. You should have about ½ cup. Blanch the peas for 1 minute, then drain. Cook the broccoli, cauliflower, zucchini, and haricots verts separately in boiling salted water for 5 minutes, drain, and combine all the cooked vegetables in a mixing bowl. Chop the tomatoes, season them with sugar, salt, and pepper, and toss them with the lemon juice, then drain. In a small bowl combine the pine nuts and bacon.

In a large skillet sauté about half the garlic in about half of the olive oil until golden. Add the broccoli, cauliflower, zucchini, haricots verts, peas, parsley, and red pepper flakes, and sauté until combined. In a separate skillet, sauté the remaining garlic in the remaining olive oil until golden. Put the tomatoes and 2 tablespoons basil on top and cook over low heat without stirring until the tomatoes soften. Combine the heavy cream and chicken broth in a small saucepan and heat gently.

Cook the spaghetti for 2 minutes in boiling salted water, then drain. In a large serving bowl toss the hot pasta with the butter, then toss in the cream mixture and the Parmigiano. Add the green vegetable mixture and about half of the tomato mixture and toss to combine. Top with the remaining tomatoes and the bacon and pine nuts. Sprinkle on the remaining 1 tablespoon basil and serve.

Serves 2

Ina Garten's Spinach and Ricotta Lasagna

I tore this recipe out of a magazine at the hairdresser's one day and my husband loved it.

8 lasagna noodles

2 (28-ounce) cans peeled whole plum tomatoes

2 tablespoons extra-virgin olive oil

1 tablespoon minced garlic

3 tablespoons chopped flat-leaf parsley

Freshly ground black pepper to taste

3 cups skim milk

6 tablespoons unsalted butter

¼ cup all-purpose flour

½ teaspoon grated nutmeg

Salt to taste

1 cup part-skim ricotta cheese

½ cup grated part-skim mozzarella cheese

Note

Always be sure to let lasagna rest and settle before serving.

Preheat the oven to 325°F. Cook the lasagna noodles in boiling water until al dente, drain, and lay flat. Drain the tomatoes and crush them by hand or with a fork.

Heat the olive oil in a heavy saucepan. Add the garlic and cook over low heat for 3 minutes. Add the drained tomatoes and 2 tablespoons of the parsley and season with pepper to taste. Raise the heat to medium and cook the tomato sauce, stirring occasionally, for 10 minutes. Set aside.

Heat the milk in a saucepan until it begins to bubble. Melt the butter in another saucepan over low heat. Add the flour to the melted butter and whisk continuously over low heat until a smooth paste forms. Pour in the hot milk and whisk constantly until the sauce thickens to the consistency of sour cream, about 3 minutes. Add the nutmeg and season with salt and pepper to taste. Remove from the heat and whisk in the ricotta.

To assemble lasagna, spread about ½ cup of the tomato sauce over the bottom of a 9 by 13-inch baking dish. Cover the sauce with 4 lasagna noodles, overlapping them slightly. Spoon half of the ricotta mixture on top of the noodles and spread it evenly with an offset spatula. Spread half of the remaining tomato sauce evenly on top of the béchamel. Cover with the remaining noodles. Repeat layers with the remaining ricotta mixture and the remaining tomato sauce.

Sprinkle the mozzarella over the lasagna. Cover loosely with foil and bake for 30 minutes. Remove the foil and bake for 15 additional minutes. Remove from the oven and sprinkle with the remaining 1 tablespoon parsley. Let the lasagna rest for 10 minutes before cutting and serving.

Serves 10 to 12

Deeda's Green Pasta with Vegetables and Bacon

This is an easy recipe I have been making for years. The green pasta mixed with all the green vegetables makes it look special.

3 zucchini, sliced ⅛-inch thick
1 tablespoon extra-virgin olive oil
3 cups frozen peas
2 cups finely chopped broccoli florets
1 cup 1 ½-inch slices haricots verts
8 ounces green angel hair pasta or
    green tagliatelle
Salt to taste
2 tablespoons unsalted butter
¾ cup crème fraîche
Freshly ground black pepper to taste
8 slices bacon, cooked very crisp
    and crumbled

Sauté the zucchini in the oil until slightly tender. Cook the peas, broccoli, and haricots verts in boiling water until just tender and drain.

Cook the pasta in salted boiling water until al dente. Drain. Toss with the butter and crème fraîche and season with salt and pepper.

Mix the peas, broccoli, haricots verts, and zucchini with the pasta and then sprinkle the crumbled bacon on top. Serve hot.

Serves 4

Chicken Pasta with Fried Croutons

This is a recipe created by our longtime cook, Elsa, who worked in our house in Washington, D.C., for more than twenty years. I could come back from Paris and describe a dish to her, and she could always easily recreate it.

2 ½ cups shredded poached chicken breast
6 ounces tagliolini or other long pasta,
    broken into ½-inch pieces, cooked
    al dente, and drained
5 tablespoons unsalted butter
2 tablespoons chopped yellow onion
1 tablespoon all-purpose flour
1 ½ cups heavy cream
½ cup chicken stock
Truffle salt to taste (optional)
¼ cup grated Parmigiano Reggiano (optional)
4 slices white bread, crusts removed

Preheat the oven to 360°F.

Combine the chicken breast and pasta in a bowl. In a small skillet, melt 1 tablespoon of the butter with the chopped onion over medium heat. Add the flour and stir until blended.

In a saucepan, bring the cream to a boil with the chicken stock and cook for 3 minutes. Add this sauce to the pasta and chicken. Stir to combine, then transfer to a baking dish. Sprinkle on truffle salt and/or Parmigiano, if using.

Bake in the preheated oven until hot and bubbling, about 15 minutes.

While the dish is in the oven, cut the bread into ⅓-inch cubes and fry them in 2 tablespoons butter. Melt the remaining 2 tablespoons butter and toss the bread cubes with it. When the chicken is hot and bubbling, scatter the bread on the surface and broil until brown and crisp.

Serves 4

POULTRY
&
MEAT

These recipes have been my favorites for many years. Most were given to me by friends; all have been a success with guests. We devour a great deal of chicken, and lately, with changing tastes, we have been adding quite a few Middle Eastern spices.

Opaque painting, pencil, and watercolor. 13 x 19 in. (33.8 x 48.5 cm).

194	Harissa-Marinated Chicken with Grapefruit Salad
195	Edita's Borscht with Brisket
196	Poulet au Gros Sel
198	Roast Chicken with Wild Rice, Orange, and Pistachio Stuffing
	Chicken Burgers
199	Chicken Divan
200	Gigot de Sept Heures
201	Louise de Vilmorin's Pot-au-Feu
	L'Escalopine de Veau au Champagne

Harissa-Marinated Chicken with Grapefruit Salad

This was inspired by a Yotam Ottolenghi recipe.

Harissa and Chicken
¼ teaspoon coriander seeds, toasted
¼ teaspoon cumin seeds, toasted
¼ teaspoon caraway seeds, toasted
1 ½ teaspoons olive oil
1 small red onion, roughly chopped
3 cloves garlic, roughly chopped
2 mild fresh red chiles, seeded, and
    roughly chopped
1 dried red chile, seeded, and roughly
    chopped
1 red bell pepper, roasted, peeled,
    and seeded
1 ½ teaspoons tomato puree
2 tablespoons freshly squeezed lemon juice
½ teaspoon salt
1 tablespoon Greek yogurt
1 whole chicken

Salad and Citrus Sauce
2 pink grapefruits
About ¼ cup pink grapefruit juice
⅓ cup freshly squeezed lemon juice
½ cup maple syrup
1 pinch ground cinnamon
Salt to taste
Leaves of 1 small head Bibb lettuce
¼ cup pistachios
1 teaspoon extra-virgin olive oil

Note
You can purchase harissa in Middle Eastern grocery stores, but making your own isn't difficult. I like to make extra and pass it on the side for real spice lovers.

Grind the coriander, cumin, and caraway seeds. Heat the olive oil in a skillet, add the onion, garlic, and fresh and dried chiles, and cook over medium heat until they turn dark, 6 to 8 minutes. In a food processor, process the spices, the bell pepper, the onion mixture, the tomato puree, the lemon juice, and the salt. Combine the paste with the yogurt and rub it all over the chicken. Place the chicken in a bowl, cover, and refrigerate for 8 hours.

Preheat the oven to 425°F. Place the chicken in a roasting pan. After 20 minutes, lower the oven temperature to 350°F and roast the chicken until an instant-read thermometer inserted into the thickest part of the leg registers 165°F, about 1 hour. Broil the chicken to char the skin in spots, 2 to 3 minutes. Let the chicken rest briefly before carving.

Peel the grapefruits and over a bowl, carve away any white pith and cut away the membranes. Set aside the supremes of grapefruit and squeeze the membranes to extract any juice. Strain this juice into a measuring cup and add enough grapefruit juice to come to ½ cup. Place the grapefruit juice, lemon juice, maple syrup, cinnamon, and salt to taste in a small saucepan and simmer to reduce to one-third of its original volume.

To serve, toss the lettuce, grapefruit segments, and pistachios with the olive oil and salt to taste. Make a bed of the salad on a platter, place the warm chicken on top, and drizzle the citrus sauce over the chicken.

Serves 4

Edita's Borscht with Brisket

Edita is the wife and partner of Vladimir Kanevsky, who makes the most exquisite flowers out of porcelain with tole leaves. Both are Russian-born and this is Edita's family recipe.

2 pounds bone-in brisket or short ribs
1 large yellow onion, quartered
1 large russet potato, peeled and cut into
 ½-inch dice
3 cups thinly sliced cabbage
2 carrots, grated
2 large beets, grated
2 tomatoes, diced
2 tablespoons tomato paste
2 tablespoons vinegar or lemon juice
2 bay leaves
Salt and freshly ground black pepper to taste
¾ cup chopped fresh dill
¾ cup chopped flat-leaf parsley
3 cloves garlic, crushed with a garlic press
1 cup sour cream

Put the meat and onion in a stockpot, add water to cover by a few inches, and bring to a boil. Lower the heat to a simmer, cover, and cook until the meat falls off the bone, 1 ½ to 2 hours.

Remove the meat from the pot, reserving the cooking liquid. Pull the meat off the bone. Remove and discard the bone and any connective tissue and excess fat. In the meantime, add the diced potato and cabbage to the pot and cook until the potato is soft, then add the carrots, beets, tomatoes, tomato paste, and vinegar. Bring to a boil, then lower the heat to a gentle simmer, cover, and simmer for 30 minutes. Cut the meat into bite-sized pieces and add it to the pot with the bay leaves. Season to taste with salt and freshly ground black pepper. Simmer for another 15 minutes. Add ½ cup of the fresh dill, the parsley, and the garlic, and remove from the heat.

You can eat this right away, but it is better if it is cooked 1 to 2 days ahead. If cooking in advance, refrigerate and the fat will rise to the top and solidify. Remove and discard excess fat.

To serve, remove and discard bay leaves, then gently reheat the soup. Ladle it into bowls and garnish with the remaining ¼ cup dill. Pass the sour cream in a bowl on the side.

Serves 4

Poulet au Gros Sel

La Grenouille is a great old New York restaurant that was a favorite of mine and Bill's. We held a few of our larger parties there, in the charming upstairs room. Even though this dish was removed from the menu a few years ago, Charles Masson, the previous owner, would graciously bring it back for our parties. We also serve it frequently at home, and we like a dab of wasabi with it.

1 whole chicken, brined and patted dry
Salt and freshly ground black pepper to taste
Peeled and turned turnips
Cauliflower florets
Broccoli florets
Baby carrots
Haricots verts, cut into 1 ½-inch slices
2 tablespoons unsalted butter
2 tablespoons all-purpose flour
2 cups chicken stock, warm
1 cup heavy cream, scalded
¼ cup prepared horseradish
1 teaspoon wasabi
Fresh herb sprigs for garnish
Coarse sea salt to taste

Preheat the oven to 350°F. Season the chicken inside and out with salt and pepper and roast until an instant-read thermometer inserted into the thickest part of the leg registers 165°F, about 1 ½ hours. Let the chicken stand at room temperature briefly before carving.

While the chicken is roasting, steam the vegetables individually. You can also steam wedges of cabbage.

In a saucepan melt the butter. Whisk in the flour. Cook over low heat for 10 minutes, stirring frequently. Do not allow to brown. Add the chicken stock in a thin stream and cook over low heat, whisking constantly, for 10 minutes. When the mixture is slightly thicker than sour cream, whisk in the cream and continue to cook, whisking constantly, until the mixture thickens again. Remove from the heat and whisk in the horseradish and wasabi.

Carve the chicken and arrange chicken and vegetables on each plate. Garnish with herbs and sprinkle generously with coarse sea salt. Serve the sauce on the side.

Serves 2 to 4

Roast Chicken with Wild Rice, Orange, and Pistachio Stuffing

I use this stuffing in roast chicken or capon. I tell guests we're having roast chicken and ask whether they prefer white, dark, or both. This is then carved in the kitchen and the wild rice is placed on the side.

1 cup wild rice
Salt and freshly ground black pepper
2 navel oranges
¾ cup golden raisins
½ cup pistachios, halved
1 whole chicken

Preheat the oven to 350°F.

Cook the rice according to package instructions. Season with salt and pepper. Thinly slice the oranges (leave the peels on). Toss the rice, orange slices, raisins, and pistachios. Taste and season with salt and pepper if needed.

Stuff the cavity of the bird with the rice mixture. Roast until an instant-read thermometer inserted into the thickest part of the leg registers 165°F, about 1 ½ hours. Let the chicken stand at room temperature briefly before carving.

Serves 4 to 6

Chicken Burgers

I've seen chicken burgers in many cookbooks, but most have too many filler ingredients for my taste. These consist mostly of chicken.

7 slices white sandwich bread, crusts
      removed
2 ½ pounds ground chicken
1 yellow onion, shredded on the largest
      holes of a box grater
Salt and freshly ground black pepper to taste
4 tablespoons unsalted butter.
½ cup heavy cream

Grind the sandwich bread into fine breadcrumbs in a food processor fitted with the metal blade. Set aside in a soup bowl. In a bowl combine the chicken and onion. Season the mixture and mix well by hand.

With wet hands shape a handful of the chicken mixture into an oval patty about 1 inch thick. (I like to make this amount of chicken into 8 smaller burgers and serve two per diner.) Dredge the burger in the breadcrumbs and press the bread crumbs lightly into the burger to coat it on all sides. Repeat with remaining chicken mixture and breadcrumbs, placing the burgers on a baking sheet.

Melt the butter in a skillet and cook the burgers until crisp and browned on the outside and cooked through in the center. Remove them to serving plates as they are cooked. Add the cream to the skillet and simmer it for a few minutes, stirring. When the cream has reduced slightly, pour it over the burgers and serve immediately.

Serves 4

Chicken Divan

This recipe comes from a long-gone New York restaurant, Divan Parisien, that my father used to take me to in the 1950s. The Chicago cookbook writer Peggy Harvey tried to get the recipe from the chef, but as it was his signature dish, he wouldn't relinquish it. Fortunately, the maître d' was more generous with her. I was thrilled when I was served this at her house, and more thrilled when she gave the recipe to me.

4 boneless skinless chicken breasts
1 (15-ounce) can chicken broth
1 rib celery
1 clove garlic
2 sprigs tarragon or parsley
Salt and freshly ground black pepper to taste
1 cup whole milk
1 bunch broccoli
6 tablespoons unsalted butter
½ cup grated Parmigiano Reggiano
2 tablespoons all-purpose flour
½ cup heavy cream
White pepper to taste
½ cup Hollandaise Sauce (page 237)

Place the chicken breasts, the broth, the celery, and the garlic in a shallow saucepan. Add the herbs and season with salt and pepper. Simmer until the chicken is cooked through. Remove the chicken and set aside. Strain the broth, discard solids, and measure 1 cup broth. Combine the 1 cup broth with the milk and heat in a small saucepan.

While the chicken is cooking, chop the broccoli into florets and slice the stalks into 1-inch pieces. Cook in boiling salted water until tender, 15 to 30 minutes. Drain and break up the florets into small pieces. Spread the broccoli in a shallow baking dish. Dot with 2 tablespoons butter and sprinkle on ¼ cup Parmigiano.

Melt 2 tablespoons butter in a small saucepan and whisk in the flour. Cook, stirring, over low heat for 10 minutes. Add the milk and broth mixture in a thin stream while stirring and continue to cook over low heat, stirring constantly, until reduced by half, about 45 minutes. Add the cream and season to taste with salt and white pepper.

Preheat the broiler with a shelf about 1 inch below it. Slice the chicken or leave it whole and arrange it on top of the broccoli. Whisk the Hollandaise into the cream sauce and pour over the chicken. Dot with the remaining 2 tablespoons butter and sprinkle with the remaining ¼ cup cheese. Broil until browned, about 3 minutes.

Serves 4

POULTRY & MEAT

I have had recipes for seven-hour roast lamb given to me by several French friends, including Liliane de Rothschild, who served it in the most beautiful large antique casserole with two of the most enormous heavy silver spoons I've ever seen. The meat falls off the bone and it is incredible. I love this dish.

14 cloves garlic
1 (5- to 6-pound) leg of lamb on the bone
¼ cup extra-virgin olive oil
Salt and freshly ground black pepper
    to taste
2 small yellow onions, thinly sliced
4 carrots
3 turnips, peeled and quartered
3 cups dry white wine

Note
We serve potato ribbons (page 210) with this and fresh shelled English peas if available, or carrot puree (page 212).

Preheat the oven to 400°F.

Thinly slice 4 of the garlic cloves. Make small incisions in the lamb and put a sliver of garlic inside each incision.

Rub the lamb well with the olive oil and season all over with salt and pepper.

Place the lamb in a Dutch oven and add the sliced onions, whole carrots, turnips, the remaining 10 garlic cloves (left whole), and the wine.

Cover the Dutch oven. Roast for 30 minutes. Reduce the heat to 350°F and roast for 30 additional minutes. Reduce the heat to 200°F. Baste occasionally and roast until the meat is extremely tender and pulls apart at the touch of a fork, 5 to 7 hours total.

Serves 6

Louise de Vilmorin's Pot-au-Feu

I went to a dinner at the novelist and journalist Louise de Vilmorin's house just outside Paris, where this was served.

4 pounds rump roast or brisket, trussed
2 yellow onions, each stuck with 2 cloves
1 bouquet garni
6 large leeks, tied in a bunch
12 small or 4 large carrots
12 small white onions
12 small or 6 large turnips
3 celery roots, peeled
1 teaspoon salt
6 large potatoes
1 large head cabbage, cut in 6 wedges
2 large marrow bones, tied in cheesecloth
Toasted thickly sliced rustic bread
    for serving

Place the meat in a large stockpot with 3 quarts of water. Bring slowly to a boil, covered, and skim any foam from the surface. Add the yellow onions stuck with cloves and the bouquet garni and simmer very gently for 1 ½ hours. Add the leeks, carrots, white onions, turnips, celery roots, and salt and simmer for another 2 hours. Boil the potatoes separately until tender. Peel and cut into quarters. Simmer the cabbage with the marrow bones in water and cover for 15 minutes.

To serve, slice the meat thickly and arrange on a platter surrounded by the vegetables. Strain the broth and pass separately. Place a slice or two of bread on each plate and allow diners to serve themselves.

Serves 6

L'Escalopine de Veau au Champagne

Veal scallops in Champagne sauce are quick to prepare but so rich and delicious.

8 very thin veal scallops
All-purpose flour for dredging
4 tablespoons unsalted butter
¾ cup Champagne
4 ounces morel mushrooms, thinly sliced
1 ½ cups heavy cream
2 teaspoons cognac
Salt and white pepper to taste

Dredge the veal scallops in flour. Melt the butter in a skillet and sauté the scallops until browned. Remove from the skillet and set aside. Add the Champagne to the skillet and simmer for 5 minutes. Add the mushrooms and the cream, and cook, stirring frequently, until the cream thickens. Add the cognac and season to taste with salt and pepper.

Add the scallops back to the skillet with the sauce and simmer for 4 minutes before serving.

Serves 2

FISH & LOBSTER

The only fish my husband Bill liked was lobster, so I experimented with a lot of lobster dishes! Serving lobster always feels quite special. I call everyone ahead of time to check whether they like lobster: After one rather disastrous evening when a guest admitted she was allergic to lobster, all I had for her at the last minute were a few scrambled eggs and lots of vegetables!

204   Lobster Tiede Surrounded with Clusters of Vegetables with Beurre Blanc

Lobster Soufflé

206   Dover Sole with Mashed Potatoes and Capers

207   Filets de Poisson en Soufflé with Sauce Mousseline

Lobster Tiede Surrounded with Clusters of Vegetables with Beurre Blanc

This is very attractive and very easy.

4 lobsters, about 1 ¼ pounds each
1 cup 3 ½-inch slices haricots verts or
    1 bunch asparagus, stems peeled
16 baby carrots
4 new potatoes, peeled and turned
1 cup broccoli florets
1 cup halved or quartered cherry tomatoes
1 cucumber, peeled and sliced
1 cup Beurre Blanc (page 236)

Note
You can use any vegetables you like: steamed cauliflower and sliced avocado with a squeeze of lemon juice are good choices as well. I usually ask the fishmonger to steam the lobster and take it out of the shell, but to clean the tail shell for me, which I use for serving.

Steam the lobsters and allow them to cool. Shell the lobsters, but keep the tail shells intact. Chop the lobster meat into bite-sized pieces and fill the tail shells with the meat. Place one tail on each of 4 serving plates.

Separately, steam the haricots verts, carrots, potatoes, and broccoli. Peel the potatoes and turn them. Place a small portion of haricots verts, carrots, potatoes, broccoli, cherry tomatoes, and cucumber slices on each plate.

Drizzle Beurre Blanc over each serving.

Serves 4

Lobster Soufflé

3 tablespoons unsalted butter, plus more
    for dish
3 tablespoons all-purpose flour, plus more
    for dish
½ cup plus 2 tablespoons light cream
½ cup chicken broth
1 cup grated Parmigiano Reggiano
6 large eggs, separated
1 pound cooked lobster meat, cut into
    bite-sized pieces
½ teaspoon paprika
½ teaspoon cream of tartar

Note
I love to top this with the Mousseline Sauce (page 236).

Preheat the oven to 350°F. Butter and flour a 2-quart soufflé dish and set aside.

In the top of a double boiler melt the 3 tablespoons butter. Whisk in the 3 tablespoons flour until perfectly smooth and cook for 1 minute. Add ½ cup cream and the chicken broth and cook, whisking constantly. As soon as the mixture begins to thicken, add the cheese. Cook, whisking constantly, until the mixture is smooth and about as thick as sour cream. Remove from the heat and beat in the 6 egg yolks. Set aside to cool.

In a bowl combine the lobster meat with 2 tablespoons of the cheese mixture and the remaining 2 tablespoons cream. Sprinkle on the paprika. Mix thoroughly and place in the prepared soufflé dish.

Beat the 6 egg whites until they are foamy, then sprinkle in the cream of tartar and beat until they form stiff peaks. Spoon about one quarter of the egg whites into the remaining cheese mixture and fold gently until well combined. Drizzle this mixture slowly over the remaining egg whites and fold gently until combined.

Pour this mixture over the lobster and bake at 350°F until puffed and browned, about 25 minutes.

Serves 6

Dover Sole with Mashed Potatoes and Capers

4 small to medium potatoes
1 stick (8 tablespoons) salted butter
3 tablespoons crème fraîche
Salt to taste
¼ cup plus 2 tablespoons capers
3 whole dover sole, skinned, boned, and
    cut into 12 filets
Freshly ground black pepper to taste
⅓ cup all-purpose flour
Juice of ½ lemon
Chopped fresh chives for garnish

Note
You can substitute halibut or branzino for
the sole if you prefer. I also make this with
truffled mashed potatoes: if you like that
idea, leave out the capers and incorporate
truffle salt and chopped truffles into the
mashed potatoes and sprinkle more truffle
on top just before serving.

Boil the potatoes until soft enough to pierce with a fork, then drain, peel, and mash with a fork or potato masher. Mash in 2 tablespoons of the butter, the crème fraîche, and salt. Fold in ¼ cup capers and beat with a whisk until creamy. Cover with foil to keep warm and set aside.

Season the filets with salt and pepper. Dredge them in the flour. Melt 2 tablespoons of the butter in a large nonstick skillet over medium-high heat until foaming. Cook the filets skin-sides first until pale golden brown, about 2 minutes. Using a fish spatula, carefully turn the filets and cook the other sides for 1 minute.

Spread ½-inch layer (no more) of mashed potatoes on warm individual serving plates. Arrange 3 filets next to each other on top of each portion of potatoes.

Melt the remaining 4 tablespoons of butter in a medium saucepan over medium heat. Add lemon juice (you can squeeze it in directly through a strainer) while swirling the saucepan. Remove the saucepan for the heat. Spoon the sauce over the sole. Garnish with the remaining 2 tablespoons capers and the chives.

Serves 4

I got this recipe from a friend over thirty years ago. We serve it on a low round platter from Chinatown that can go in the oven or in an oblong Pyrex dish with a rattan holder. (Sometimes I think everything in this house—except the plumbing—is rattan or rush!)

3 tablespoons unsalted butter, plus more
    for platter
½ cup dry white wine
1 tablespoon minced shallot
8 ounces skinless flounder or sole filets
1 cup whole milk
3 tablespoons all-purpose flour
Salt and freshly ground black pepper to taste
1 egg yolk
5 egg whites
½ cup coarsely grated Swiss cheese
2 cups Mousseline Sauce (page 236)

Preheat the oven to 425°F with a rack in the upper third. Butter an ovenproof platter about 16 inches long and set aside.

Place the wine and shallot in a skillet, bring to a simmer, and poach the fish filets for 6 minutes. Remove the filets with a slotted spatula (it doesn't matter if they break apart). Strain the poaching liquid into a 2½-quart saucepan and simmer briskly until it has reduced to ¼ cup. Meanwhile, place the milk in a small saucepan and bring to a simmer.

Add the 3 tablespoons butter to the reduced poaching liquid, wait for it to melt, and then whisk in the flour. Cook, whisking constantly, for 2 minutes. Remove the saucepan from the heat and beat in the hot milk. Season with salt and pepper. Return to the heat and cook, stirring, for 1 minute with the mixture simmering. Remove the pan from the heat and beat in the egg yolk. Check and adjust seasoning, if necessary.

Beat the egg whites with a pinch of salt to stiff peaks. Fold about one quarter of the egg whites into the milk mixture. Set aside about 2 tablespoons of the cheese and fold the remaining cheese into the milk mixture as well. Gently fold in the remaining egg whites.

Spread a ¼-inch layer of the mixture in the bottom of the prepared platter. Flake the poached fish filets on top. Spoon the rest of the mixture over the fish. Sprinkle on the reserved 2 tablespoons cheese. Bake in the upper third of the preheated oven until the soufflé has puffed and browned on top, 15 to 18 minutes. Pass Mousseline Sauce on the side when serving.

Serves 6

Watercolor, opaque painting, and pencil, 13 ½ x 19 in. (34 x 48.6 cm).

VEGETABLES

These side dishes are easy to make but very delicious and always impress and delight guests. They are also versatile, pairing fairly well with nearly any main course.

210   Fried Potato Ribbons
         Crushed New Potatoes
212   Jayne's Cauliflower with Puree of Peas
         Carrot Puree
213   Wild Rice with Grapes and Pecans
         Potato and Artichoke Gratin

Fried Potato Ribbons

I don't know where I got this recipe—I probably tore it from a magazine—but it is a longtime favorite. To whomever created this recipe, I am very grateful to you, because these are deliciously addictive!

3 large white potatoes, about 1 ½ pounds
Vegetable oil for frying
Coarse salt to taste

Prepare a bowl of ice water. Line a baking sheet with paper towels. Peel the potatoes and with a mandoline slice them lengthwise into thin strips ½ inch wide and place in the ice water. Soak the potatoes for 15 minutes, drain them, and pat them dry.

Place 2 inches of oil in an electric fryer or deep, heavy pot and bring to 350°F. Fry the potatoes, working in batches, until just golden, about 1 minute. Remove with a slotted spoon to the prepared baking sheet. Wait for the oil to reach 350°F again before adding the next batch. Sprinkle the potatoes generously with salt and serve piping hot.

Serves 4

Crushed New Potatoes

12 new potatoes
3 tablespoons extra-virgin olive oil
2 tablespoons unsalted butter, melted
Salt and freshly ground black pepper to taste
Chopped fresh rosemary to taste

Note
You can use thyme or rosemary or other herbs in place of, or in addition to, the rosemary if you like.

Bring a pot of salted water to a boil. Add the potatoes and cook them until they are tender enough to pierce with a fork. Drain.

Preheat the oven to 450°F. Brush a sheet pan with about half of the olive oil. Place the potatoes on the sheet pan, leaving plenty of room between them. With a potato masher, gently press down on a potato until it slightly mashes, then cut it into quarters, leaving the skin on the bottom intact. Rotate the potato masher 90 degrees and mash again. Repeat with remaining potatoes. Brush the tops of the crushed potatoes with the remaining olive oil and the butter. Season with salt and pepper and sprinkle on the rosemary.

Bake until golden brown, 20 to 25 minutes.

Serves 6

VEGETABLES

This is a dish I had at Jayne Wrightsman's. She generously obliged my many requests for her recipes, but this is one I go back to the most.

1 head cauliflower

2 cups frozen peas

½ clove garlic, crushed

About 1 cup half and half

Salt and freshly ground black pepper to taste

Small croutons for garnish

Steam the cauliflower until tender enough to pierce with a paring knife but still firm. Break into florets and slice the stem.

Cook the peas in boiling water until soft, then drain. In a blender combine the peas and garlic and puree until smooth. Gradually drizzle in half and half until the sauce has the consistency you prefer. Taste and adjust seasoning.

Place the cooked cauliflower on a serving tray and pour the puree over it. Garnish with croutons.

Serves 4

Carrot Puree

8 ounces (about 3 medium) carrots, halved lengthwise and chopped into ½-inch pieces

1 small clove garlic

⅓ cup low-sodium chicken broth

¼ teaspoon salt

2 tablespoons heavy cream

1 tablespoon unsalted butter

Place the carrots, garlic, broth, and salt in a 1- to 2-quart heavy saucepan and simmer, covered, until carrots are very tender, 12 to 14 minutes. Puree the mixture with the cream and butter in a food processor fitted with the metal blade (or use an immersion blender) until smooth.

Serves 2

Note

This puree can be made up to one day ahead. Reheat it in an ovenproof dish, covered with foil, in a 425°F oven for 5 to 10 minutes.

Wild Rice with Grapes and Pecans

I much prefer wild rice to white rice. When my father would come home with
ducks from shooting, we would always have them with wild rice.

6 tablespoons unsalted butter
1 ½ cups wild rice
20 seedless green grapes, halved
½ cup chopped pecans
Salt and freshly ground black pepper to taste

Melt 3 tablespoons of the butter in a heavy saucepan. Add the wild
rice and mix to combine. Stir in 3 cups of water. Bring to a gentle
simmer. Cover and cook over low heat, stirring occasionally, until
rice is tender and all the water has been absorbed, 50 to 60 minutes.
Check frequently, and if the pot looks dry before the rice is fully
cooked and expanded add a few tablespoons of water at a time.

Melt the remaining 3 tablespoons butter in a skillet. Add the grapes
and the pecans and cook, stirring, until just heated through. Add the
grape and pecans to the cooked wild rice, season with salt and
pepper, mix thoroughly, and serve.

Serves 4

Potato and Artichoke Gratin

This is fantastic—the artichokes really elevate a potato gratin. Bill loved potato
gratin and once I had the idea to include artichokes in it, I loved it, too.

1 tablespoon unsalted butter, plus more
     for dish
½ cup chopped yellow onion
1 ½ cloves garlic, minced
1 pound russet potatoes, peeled and sliced
     ¼-inch thick
Salt and freshly ground black pepper to taste
4 artichoke hearts, sliced ¼ inch thick
¾ cup whipping cream
¾ cup half and half

Preheat oven to 400°F. Butter a baking dish and set aside.

Melt the 1 tablespoon butter in skillet over medium-high heat. Add the
onion and garlic and sauté until softened. Spread the onion mixture
in the bottom of the prepared baking dish. Top with half of the potatoes,
overlapping slightly if necessary. Season generously with salt and
pepper. Arrange half of the artichoke slices over the potatoes.

Repeat with the remaining potatoes, more salt and pepper, and the
remaining artichokes. Pour the cream and half and half over the gratin.

Bake in the preheated oven until potatoes are tender, about 1 hour.
Allow to set and cool slightly before serving.

Serves 4

214

CAKES, TARTS, SOUFFLÉS & COOKIES

I have a serious passion for desserts! I often start my menu planning by choosing the dessert, and even in a restaurant I look at desserts first. These are not diet desserts, but they are not heavy, either—I lust for them all. I always take a first and sometimes a second helping!

216 Richard Sax's Chocolate Cloud Cake
Chocolate Leaves
218 Deeda's Chocolate Almond Roll
Runny Crusty Chocolate Soufflé
219 Pecan Meringue Torte with Raspberries and Raspberry Sauce
Apple Pecan Crisp
220 Frozen Lemon Soufflé
Almond Meringue
222 Thin Oatmeal and Orange Cookies
Swedish Spice Cookies
223 Dora's Lace Cookies
Jayne's Chocolate Madeleines
224 Blueberry and Blackberry Tart
Carrot Cake with Orange Zest

Richard Sax's Chocolate Cloud Cake

The late writer and cooking instructor Richard Sax is the godfather of the chocolate cloud cake.

8 ounces bittersweet chocolate, coarsely
    chopped
1 stick (8 tablespoons) unsalted butter,
    at room temperature and cut into
    tablespoons
6 large eggs
1 cup sugar
1 tablespoon cognac
Finely grated zest of 1 orange
1 ½ cups heavy cream, very cold
3 tablespoons confectioners' sugar
1 teaspoon vanilla extract
Unsweetened cocoa powder for finishing

Note
The website Food52 features an excellent instructional video along with his recipe.

Heat the oven to 350°F with a rack in the center. Line the bottom of an 8-inch springform pan with a parchment circle.

Place the chocolate in a large heatproof bowl and place the bowl over boiling water (not touching the water) until it melts. When the chocolate is melted, remove from the heat and whisk in the butter 1 tablespoon at a time until smooth.

Separate 4 of the eggs. In a large bowl, whisk 2 whole eggs and 4 egg yolks with ½ cup of the sugar just until combined. Slowly whisk in the warm chocolate mixture. Whisk in the cognac and the orange zest. Separately, beat the 4 egg whites until foamy, about 2 minutes. Add the remaining ½ cup sugar and beat until soft peaks form. Fold about one quarter of the beaten egg whites into the chocolate mixture, then fold in the remaining whites. Scrape the batter into the prepared pan and smooth the top.

Set the pan on a baking sheet and bake in the preheated oven until the top is puffed and cracked and the center is no longer wobbly, 35 to 40 minutes. Let the cake cool in the pan on a rack. The center of the cake will sink.

Whip the cream, confectioners' sugar, and vanilla in a large bowl until soft peaks form. Using a spatula, fill the sunken center of the cake with the whipped cream, swirling the cream to the edges of the sunken portion. Dust lightly with cocoa powder.

Run the tip of a knife around the edge of the cake, then unbuckle the sides of the pan and remove the ring.

Serves 6 to 8

Chocolate Leaves

These make a pretty decoration.

Very good semisweet chocolate, chopped
Assorted small fresh leaves, like ivy, oak,
    or gingko, rinsed and patted dry

In the top of a double boiler set over hot, but not boiling, water, melt the chocolate, stirring until smooth. Remove the pan from the heat and let the chocolate cool slightly, stirring occasionally. With a table knife, spread about ⅓-inch melted chocolate over the back of each leaf, and place the leaves, chocolate sides up, on a plate. Refrigerate the leaves until the chocolate hardens, and then carefully peel away the leaves from the chocolate.

Deeda's Chocolate Almond Roll

One day I had the notion to put slivered almonds into a chocolate roll, and it really just transformed it. The cognac certainly doesn't hurt!

Roll
Butter for pan
Flour for pan
4 large eggs
⅔ cup sugar
2 tablespoons cocoa powder
2 teaspoons baking powder
2 tablespoons potato starch

Filling
1 ½ cups heavy cream
1 tablespoon sugar
2 tablespoons vanilla extract
1 tablespoon cognac
¼ cup slivered almonds
Powdered sugar for finishing

Preheat the oven to 450°F. Line a jellyroll pan with wax paper. Butter and flour the wax paper.

Whip the eggs and sugar together until light and airy. In a small bowl sift together the cocoa powder, baking powder, and potato starch. Add the dry mixture to the egg mixture and combine thoroughly.

Spread the mixture (trying not to deflate it) evenly into the prepared pan. Bake until just firm, about 5 minutes, then remove and allow to cool. Flip the roll out of the pan onto a kitchen towel with another sheet of waxed paper on top of it. Peel off the wax paper that was underneath while it was baking.

Whip the cream to soft peaks. Add the sugar and vanilla and beat until stiff peaks form. Fold in the cognac. Spread the whipped cream on top of the chocolate roll. Sprinkle on the almonds.

Using the wax paper and detaching it as you go, roll into a log. Sprinkle with powdered sugar and serve.

Serves 6

Runny Crusty Chocolate Soufflé

4 ounces unsweetened chocolate
3 tablespoons unsalted butter
3 tablespoons all-purpose flour
1 ½ cups whole milk, scalded
¾ cup plus 2 tablespoons sugar
2 tablespoons hot water
6 large eggs, separated
3 tablespoons cognac
2 egg whites

Note
I often serve this with 1 cup of cognac-flavored whipped cream mixed with 10 to 12 tablespoons of vanilla ice cream. Scoop out spoonfuls of the ice cream in advance, put them on a plate, and freeze them until just the last moment, then mix them with the whipped cream just before the soufflé comes out of the oven.

Melt the chocolate in the top of a double boiler. Melt the butter in a small saucepan. Whisk in the flour and cook, whisking constantly, until smooth. Add the milk in a thin stream, still whisking constantly, and continue cooking until thickened to the consistency of sour cream. Whisk in ¾ cup of the sugar and the hot water.

In a large bowl beat the 6 egg yolks until light in color. Whisk in the warm milk mixture, then the melted chocolate. Whisk until cooled, then whisk in the cognac.

Preheat the oven to 385°F.

Just before baking, beat the 8 egg whites until very stiff. Stir about one quarter of the egg whites into the yolk mixture, then gently fold in the remaining whites. Pour the mixture into an unbuttered 10¾-inch round porcelain baking dish with ½-inch sides. Sprinkle the remaining 2 tablespoons sugar on top and bake until the crust is firm and the center still very soft but not wobbly, 12 to 15 minutes.

Serves 6

Pecan Meringue Torte with Raspberries and Raspberry Sauce

This may not sound incredible or compelling, but it is absolutely sensational. It is also quick to assemble at the last minute.

Butter for pan
All-purpose flour for pan
2 egg whites
½ cup plus 1 tablespoon sugar
½ teaspoon vanilla extract
½ cup chopped pecans
½ cup heavy cream
1 pint vanilla ice cream, softened
3 to 6 ounces fresh raspberries
1 cup Raspberry Sauce (page 238)

Note
I like to make just one meringue and arrange the filling on top, but you can also double the ingredients and make two 8-inch diameter meringues and layer the raspberries and ice cream in between—a very high, glamorous, grand-looking dessert.

Preheat the oven to 325°F. Butter and flour an 8-inch round cake pan and set aside.

Beat the egg whites in a large bowl until foamy. Continue beating until very stiff, adding ½ cup of the sugar gradually. Beat in the vanilla extract. Fold in the chopped pecans. Spoon the meringue into the prepared pan. Spread the meringue up the side and smooth the top—the cooked meringue should have a raised border to contain the ice cream, whipped cream, and raspberries. Bake until firm, about 45 minutes. Cool the meringue completely in the pan on a rack, then carefully unmold.

Whip the cream to soft peaks with the remaining 1 tablespoon sugar. Spread the softened ice cream on top of the meringue. Spread the whipped cream on top of the ice cream. Top with the fresh raspberries and raspberry sauce. Serve immediately.

Serves 4 to 6

Apple Pecan Crisp

A classic for a reason, this is eminently flexible and adaptable.

Filling
Butter for pan
½ cup golden raisins
½ cup sliced dried apricots
¼ cup bourbon
4 to 6 cups ½-inch slices Granny Smith
    or other tart apples
Juice of 1 lemon
½ cup jarred pitted sour cherries in syrup
3 tablespoons julienned orange zest
2 tablespoons apricot jam

Topping
1 cup all-purpose flour
½ cup granulated sugar
¼ cup light brown sugar
2 teaspoons ground cinnamon
1 pinch salt
1 ½ sticks (12 tablespoons) unsalted butter,
    cold, and cut into tablespoons
1 cup chopped pecans

Preheat the oven to 350°F. Butter a large baking dish (I use a 9- or 10-inch round ceramic quiche pan with 1 ¾-inch sides) and set aside.

Plump the raisins and apricots in the bourbon. Drain any excess liquid. Sprinkle the apple slices with the lemon juice and toss with raisins and apricots, cherries, and zest. Stir in the apricot jam and spread evenly in the prepared baking dish.

For the topping, in a food processor fitted with the metal blade, pulse the flour with both types of sugar, cinnamon, and salt. Add the butter and pulse until the mixture resembles wet sand, and then stir in the pecans. Sprinkle the topping over the filling and bake until the topping is golden and apples are soft, 35 to 40 minutes.

Serves 6

Frozen Lemon Soufflé

A favorite with guests, this is wonderful plain, but it is sensational with the Almond Meringue incorporated as two interior layers (not on top).

1 ½ cups sugar

1 tablespoon light corn syrup

8 egg yolks

2 large eggs

Finely grated zest and juice of 3 lemons

2 cups heavy cream, chilled

2 disks Almond Meringue (optional,
    see below)

Candied orange peel for garnish

Note
This can be made one or two days in advance, but garnish with the candied peel just before serving. This can also be made in eight individual 1-cup soufflé dishes.

Put a parchment-paper or greased heavy aluminum foil collar around a 2-quart soufflé dish (6 ¾ inches in diameter and 2 ½ inches high) and secure with tape. The collar should extend 2 ½ inches above the rim.

Combine the sugar, corn syrup, and 1 cup water in a saucepan and bring to a boil. Cover and cook for 5 minutes. Uncover and boil to the hardball stage (260°F on a candy thermometer).

With an electric mixer, beat the egg yolks and whole eggs until pale and fluffy, 7 to 8 minutes. When the syrup is ready and still hot, drizzle it in a thin stream down the side of the bowl into the eggs while beating constantly and beat until the bottom of the bowl is cool. Beat in the lemon zest and juice.

In a separate bowl, whip the cream to firm peaks, then fold the cream into the lemon mixture. Transfer the mixture to the soufflé dish. (If using the Almond Meringue, spread about one third of the soufflé mixture evenly in the prepared pan using an offset spatula. Top with one disk of meringue, either whole or crushed by hand. Spread half of the remaining soufflé mixture on top. Top with the second disk of meringue. Then spread the remaining soufflé mixture on top of the second layer of meringue.) The dish should be filled at least halfway up the collar. Smooth the top.

Freeze for at least 8 hours. Remove the collar and decorate with candied peel. To facilitate serving, remove from freezer and put in refrigerator for 20 minutes before scooping onto individual dessert plates.

Serves 8

Almond Meringue

5 egg whites

¼ teaspoon cream of tartar

1 cup superfine sugar

1 ½ cups blanched almond flour

Note
The baked layer can be frozen and makes a good emergency dessert when filled with fruit and whipped cream or ice cream.

Place an oven rack in the lowest position. Preheat the oven to 200°F. Trace two equal-sized circles 5 ½ inches in diameter on two pieces of parchment paper. Overturn the paper on two half-sheet pans and set aside.

Beat the egg whites to soft peaks. While still beating, add the cream of tartar and then gradually add the sugar. Beat until the whites are shiny and hold stiff peaks. Fold in the almond flour. With a spatula, divide the meringue between the two pans, spreading it to fill the circles as neatly and evenly as possible.

Bake until the meringues just start to color, about 15 minutes, then turn off the oven and allow the meringues to cool for at least 4 hours in the oven. (You can leave them overnight.)

Makes 2 large disks

Thin Oatmeal and Orange Cookies

2 ½ sticks (20 tablespoons) unsalted
    butter, at room temperature
1 cup firmly packed brown sugar
¼ cup granulated sugar
2 large eggs
2 teaspoons vanilla extract
1 ½ cups all-purpose flour
1 teaspoon baking soda
½ teaspoon salt
1 teaspoon ground cinnamon
2 tablespoons fine julienne of orange zest
3 cups quick oats
1 cup chopped pecans

Note
We make these cookies extremely thin.

Preheat the oven to 375°F.

Beat the butter and sugars until creamy. Beat in the eggs and vanilla. In a small bowl whisk together the flour, baking soda, salt, cinnamon, and orange zest. Add the dry ingredients to the butter mixture and beat to combine. Stir in the oats and pecans with a rubber spatula until well combined. Drop by rounded teaspoonfuls on ungreased cookie sheets, leaving about 3 inches between each. With the palm of your hand, press each spoonful of batter down so it is very thin and flat and about 3 inches wide. Bake until crisp, 10 to 11 minutes. Cool the cookies on the pans on a rack for 1 minute, then carefully use a thin metal spatula to remove to wire racks and allow to cool completely.

Makes about 55 cookies

Swedish Spice Cookies

These are tissue-paper thin, but you do need a lot of patience!

¼ cup dark corn syrup
1 ½ cups brown sugar
1 cup shortening
1 teaspoon baking soda
½ teaspoon ground cloves
½ teaspoon ground cinnamon
½ teaspoon ground ginger
2 teaspoons finely grated orange zest
3 ¼ to 3 ½ cups all-purpose flour, plus more
    for surface and cutters

In a medium saucepan, combine the corn syrup and brown sugar with ½ cup water. Bring to a boil. Remove the saucepan from the heat and stir in the shortening, baking soda, spices, and orange zest.

Allow the mixture to cool completely. Add flour gradually until the mixture forms a moist dough that is dry enough to roll out. Form into a disk, wrap in plastic, and refrigerate for 8 hours.

When you're read to bake the cookies, preheat the oven to 375°F. Line cookie sheets with parchment paper.

Flour a work surface. Cut off some of the dough (refrigerate the remainder) and roll it out extremely thin—the thickness of tissue paper. Flour the rolling pin as needed. Use floured cookie cutters to cut out cookies and transfer them to the prepared pans. Bake until crisp, 4 to 6 minutes. Continue with the remaining dough. Combine scraps and refrigerate until firm, then reroll and cut. Any time the dough feels too soft to handle, refrigerate it until it firms up. Cool cookies on the pans on a rack.

Makes several dozen, but the exact number depends on the size of the cutter

Dora's Lace Cookies

These are the delicious cookies of one of the wonderful cooks who would come to help us when we had parties in Washington.

1 cup light or dark corn syrup
4 tablespoons unsalted butter
¼ cup shortening
⅔ cup brown sugar
1 cup sifted all-purpose flour
1 cup ground nuts

Preheat the oven to 325°F.

Place the corn syrup, butter, shortening, and sugar in a medium saucepan and bring to a boil. Remove from the heat and stir in the flour and nuts in small additions, stirring to combine between additions.

Drop the mixture by rounded spoonfuls 3 inches apart (they spread significantly) onto nonstick cookie sheets. Bake in the preheated oven until light brown, 8 to 10 minutes. Cool on the pans on racks for 1 minute, then use a very thin metal spatula to remove the cookies from the pans and roll them into cones while they are still warm.

Makes about 30 cookies, depending on size of spoon

Jayne's Chocolate Madeleines

I'd never had a chocolate madeleine before being served these wonderful ones at Jayne Wrightsman's, so of course I begged her for the recipe.

1 stick (8 tablespoons) unsalted butter,
    cut into cubes, at room temperature,
    plus more for pans
2 large eggs, separated
½ cup sugar
½ cup Dutch cocoa powder
½ cup sifted all-purpose flour
1 teaspoon baking powder
1 pinch salt
1 teaspoon vanilla extract

Preheat the oven to 425°F. Brush madeleine molds with butter and set aside.

In a large bowl, beat the egg yolks, sugar, and cocoa powder together. Combine the flour, baking powder, and salt in a small bowl, then fold this dry mixture into the egg yolk mixture. Beat in the 1 stick butter and vanilla. In a separate bowl, beat the egg whites to stiff peaks. Fold about one quarter of the egg whites into the egg yolk mixture, then gently fold in the remaining egg whites.

Fill each shell in the molds about ⅔ full. Bake in the preheated oven until risen and firm, checking for doneness after 5 minutes, though they will probably take 10 to 15 minutes. Turn them out of the pans and cool on a wire rack.

Makes 22 to 24 cookies

Blueberry and Blackberry Tart

2 pints blueberries
1 pint blackberries
⅔ cup sugar
2 tablespoons arrowroot or cornstarch
3 tablespoons julienned orange zest
1 baked 9-inch tart shell

Note
In this tart the berries are held in place
by a delicious puree. It works well with
strawberries and raspberries as well.
You can make the puree far in advance,
but do not put the pie together until just
before serving.

Combine ¾ cup berries and ¼ cup water in a small saucepan and cook
until soft. Put them through a food mill or force them through a sieve.
Combine the resulting puree with the sugar and arrowroot. Return to
the saucepan and cook over medium heat until the mixture is quite
thick, 1 to 2 minutes. Chill until completely cooled.

Toss the remaining berries with the orange zest, then gently fold the
berries into the puree using a spatula. Ensure that each whole berry is
coated. Pour the mixture into the shell and serve immediately.

Serves 6

Carrot Cake with Orange Zest

I adapted this from a Martha Stewart recipe.

¾ cup neutral vegetable oil, plus more
    for pan
1 cup sugar
1 tablespoon plus 2 ¼ teaspoons hot water
3 large eggs, separated
1 ¼ cups sifted cake flour
1 ¼ teaspoons ground cinnamon
¼ teaspoon salt
¾ teaspoon baking soda
¼ cup golden raisins
¾ cup chopped walnuts
¾ cup grated carrot
¼ cup finely grated orange zest
¼ cup chopped candied orange peel

Preheat the oven to 350°F. Oil a 9-inch round cake pan and set aside.

Combine the ¾ cup oil, sugar, hot water, and egg yolks. Beat on low
speed until well-combined.

Sift together flour, cinnamon, salt, and baking soda. In a separate
bowl, combine the raisins, walnuts, carrot, and orange zest.
Add about one third of the flour mixture to the yolk mixture and beat
until combined, then add about half of the carrot mixture and beat
until combined. Add about half of the remaining flour mixture and
beat until combined, then add the remaining carrot mixture and beat
until combined. Finally, add the remaining flour mixture. Beat until
combined, and then dig up from the bottom with a rubber spatula to
ensure that no dry ingredients remain at the bottom of the bowl.

In a clean bowl, beat the egg whites until they form stiff peaks.
Fold the egg whites into the batter. Pour the batter into the prepared
pan and bake until a tester inserted in the center emerges clean,
25 to 35 minutes.

Let the cake cool in the pan for about 10 minutes, then unmold and
cool completely on a wire rack. Decorate with candied orange peel
before serving.

Serves 6 to 8

ICE CREAM, SORBETS & FRUIT DESSERTS

These are cold desserts, several of which are made with fresh fruit. Be sure to reach for them in season when the grapes, berries, and peaches are at their peak. Peaches are one of my favorites—there can never be too many peaches! But the green grape mold is one of my most frequently requested recipes. An electric ice cream maker is such a help, I highly recommend it.

228	Vanilla Ice Cream with Raspberry Puree in Pot de Crème Pots
	Green Grape Sorbet
	Fresh Peach Ice Cream with Apricot Sauce
230	Anela's Poached Fresh Apple with Walnuts and Honey
	Compote of Fresh Oranges and Grapes
231	Fresh Pineapple Sherbet
	Vesuvius Ice Cream Mold with Chocolate Lace
	Sorbet à la Banane
232	Green Grape Mold with Custard Sauce
	Jayne's Watermelon Sorbet with Chocolate "Seeds"

Vanilla Ice Cream with Raspberry Puree in Pot de Crème Pots

1 cup Raspberry Sauce (page 238)
1 pint vanilla ice cream, softened

Note
Layering the ice cream and sauce makes
this special. I always use Häagen-Dazs
vanilla ice cream.

In each of four small pot de crème pots (or ramekins or cups), make a thick layer of raspberry sauce at the bottom and spread smooth. Divide the ice cream among the four dishes and spread smooth, then top each portion with the remaining raspberry sauce. Freeze, but let sit at room temperature for 30 minutes or so before serving.

Serves 4

Green Grape Sorbet

3 ½ pounds green grapes
About 1 cup sugar
About 1 teaspoon freshly squeezed
        lemon juice

Note
We use an electric sorbet maker for this,
but you can also freeze the mixture in
ice-cube trays, then remove the cubes
from the trays and follow the instructions
for serving.

Wash the grapes and puree them in a blender on high speed, working quickly to keep them from oxidizing. Strain the juice through a fine sieve and measure it. For each quart of juice, add 1 cup sugar and 1 teaspoon lemon. Taste and adjust sugar.

Process in a sorbet maker following the manufacturer's instructions. Store the sorbet in the freezer, but to serve, chop it into chunks and whip it in a blender or a food processor fitted with the metal blade, then freeze for 1 hour, scoop, and serve.

Serves 4 to 6

Fresh Peach Ice Cream with Apricot Sauce

Ice Cream
8 ripe peaches, peeled and pitted
1 ½ cups heavy cream
½ cup sugar
⅓ cup peach liqueur
Juice of 1 lemon
1 teaspoon vanilla extract
2 egg yolks

Sauce
½ cup apricot preserves
Juice of ½ lemon

Note
This is also delicious with sliced fresh
peaches and candied orange peel.

Puree the peaches in a blender. Combine with the cream, sugar, liqueur, lemon juice, vanilla, and egg yolks. Process in an ice cream maker according to the manufacturer's instructions. Store the ice cream in the freezer, but to serve, chop it into chunks and whip it in a blender or a food processor fitted with the metal blade, then freeze for a short time.

For the apricot sauce, force the preserves through a strainer, then whisk together with the lemon juice and ¼ cup hot water. Pour over scoops of ice cream.

Serves 6

Anela's Poached Fresh Apple with Walnuts and Honey

This has a surprisingly complex flavor for a dessert made with such simple ingredients.

2 cups plus 1 tablespoon sugar
1 lemon
4 Golden Delicious apples
1 cup heavy cream
2 tablespoons honey
1 /4 cups chopped walnuts

In a medium pot, combine 4 cups of water with 2 cups of the sugar. Shave 4 strips of zest off of the lemon with a vegetable peeler and add them to the pot, then squeeze the lemon's juice into the pot as well. Bring the liquid to a boil.

Peel and core the apples, leaving them intact. Add the apples to the boiling liquid and simmer until soft, turning them frequently, 6 to 8 minutes. Make sure not to overcook the apples. They should be soft but not soggy. Remove the apples with a strainer or slotted spoon and let them cool. Let the liquid simmer briskly until it thickens and turns an orange-red color, 1 additional hour.

Meanwhile, whip the cream to soft peaks. Add the remaining 1 tablespoon sugar and whip until incorporated. In a small bowl, fold the honey into about half of the whipped cream mixture (about 3 tablespoons). Fold in 1 cup of the walnuts. Fill the hole in the center of each cored apple with this mixture and refrigerate them for 2 hours. Cover and refrigerate the remaining whipped cream as well.

To serve, make pools of the reduced liquid on individual serving plates. Place an apple on each plate and top each apple with some of the remaining whipped cream. Sprinkle on the remaining ¼ cup walnuts and serve.

Serves 4

Compote of Fresh Oranges and Grapes

This is almost too simple, but it is so light and delicious.

6 navel oranges (unpeeled)
4 ounces seedless green grapes
1 cup plus 2 tablespoons sugar
Juice of 1 lemon
1 tablespoon Cointreau

Note
Sometimes we scatter chopped pistachios on each serving.

Place the oranges in a large heatproof bowl. Pour over boiling water to cover and allow to stand for 5 minutes. Drain the oranges, score the skins in quarters, and peel. Cut off any white pith, leaving only the fine skin covering the segments. Using a sharp knife, slice the oranges thinly. Place the orange slices and any juice in a serving bowl. Halve the grapes and add them to the orange slices.

In a small saucepan combine the sugar with ½ cup water. Cook, stirring, over low heat until the sugar has dissolved. Bring to a boil and boil for 1 minute, then remove from the heat and stir in the lemon juice. Allow the liquid to cool for 5 minutes and stir in the Cointreau.

Pour the syrup over the fruit and chill. Serve very cold.

Serves 6

Fresh Pineapple Sherbet

2 cups chopped pineapple
1 cup sugar

If you like a smooth sorbet, puree the pineapple in a blender, force through a sieve, and discard solids. If you like a chunky sorbet, chop it finely but leave the solids.

Combine 3 cups water and the sugar in a medium saucepan and bring to a boil. Boil, stirring, until the sugar dissolves. Remove from the heat and allow to cool.

Process the syrup and the fruit in a food processor fitted with the metal blade until smooth, working in batches if necessary. Cover and chill for 2 hours.

Process the mixture in a sorbet maker following the manufacturer's instructions.

Serves 4 to 6

Vesuvius Ice Cream Mold with Chocolate Lace

1 ½ quarts vanilla ice cream
3 ounces bittersweet chocolate, finely grated
3 ½ ounces chocolate lace

Note
This is also good with coffee ice cream.
Chocolate lace is sold in 7-ounce boxes.
I buy it at Grace's Marketplace.

Fill a 1-quart conical mold with the ice cream and freeze. About 30 minutes before serving, hollow out the center of the mold from the bottom. Fill the hollowed out space with the grated chocolate. Cover the bottom with about ½ inch of ice cream to contain the chocolate. Freeze until serving.

Just before serving, break the chocolate lace into pieces—we like to leave them fairly large. Unmold the ice cream and decorate with the lace, then serve immediately.

Serves 6

Sorbet à la Banane

2 pounds peeled bananas (not too ripe)
5 rings canned pineapple, drained
3 ¼ cups confectioners' sugar
Juice of 2 oranges
Juice of 2 lemons
½ cup crème fraîche

Note
This is wonderful with the apricot sauce
on page 228.

In a blender, puree the bananas and pineapple. Add the sugar, orange and lemon juices, and crème fraîche. Puree to combine thoroughly. Transfer to a bowl, cover, and refrigerate for 8 hours.

Process the mixture in a sorbet maker following the manufacturer's instructions.

Serves 4 to 5

Green Grape Mold with Custard Sauce

Mold
¾ cup sugar
2 envelopes unflavored gelatin powder
2 cups white wine
1 ½ pounds (about 4 cups) seedless
    green grapes

Custard Sauce
¾ cup half and half
3 egg yolks
2 tablespoons sugar
1 teaspoon vanilla extract
⅔ cup heavy cream, whipped

Note
We use Louis Jadot Pouilly-Fuissé for
the wine in this refreshing dessert, but
it's the grapes that are key, so always try
to sample them. We prefer small green
seedless grapes if they are sweet. If the
only grapes you can find are large, cut them
in half. This can be made in many different
forms of decorative molds.

For the mold, in a large saucepan, combine the sugar and gelatin. Add 1 cup water and cook over low heat, stirring constantly, until sugar and gelatin have dissolved. Stir in the wine. Place the grapes in a 6-cup ring mold, pour in the gelatin mixture, and refrigerate until set, 4 to 5 hours.

For the sauce, in a heavy saucepan, heat the half and half until bubbles form around the edge. In a small bowl, beat the egg yolks and sugar. Add about one third of the hot half and half to the yolk mixture in a thin stream, stirring constantly. Pour all of the warmed egg mixture back into the heated half and half in a thin stream, stirring constantly. Cook over low heat, stirring constantly, until thick, about 15 minutes. Transfer the mixture to a bowl and cover with waxed paper pressed against the surface. Refrigerate until thoroughly chilled. Stir in the vanilla and fold in the whipped cream.

To serve, quickly dip the underside of the mold in warm water. Invert a platter over the top of the mold, then invert both mold and platter and lift off mold. Serve custard sauce alongside the mold.

Serves 6 to 8

Jayne's Watermelon Sorbet with Chocolate "Seeds"

Jayne Wrightsman serves this in the carved-out watermelon rind, which requires either a lot of patience or an excellent chef. Sometimes guests confuse the chocolate "seeds" for actual seeds!

½ watermelon
1 cup sugar
2 tablespoons freshly squeezed lemon juice
2 tablespoons freshly squeezed orange juice
1 ounce bittersweet chocolate
½ teaspoon neutral vegetable oil

Scoop out the watermelon (leaving the rind intact if you plan to use it for serving) and roughly chop the fruit. Pick out and discards the seeds. Puree the pulp in a blender and strain through a fine sieve. You should have about 1 quart of liquid. Stir in the sugar and lemon and orange juices.

Let the mixture stand for a few minutes, stirring occasionally, to melt the sugar, then process in a sorbet maker according to the manufacturer's instructions.

While the sorbet is being processed, melt the chocolate on top of a double boiler and stir in the oil. Spread a piece of wax paper on the counter and use a small spoon to drop dots of melted chocolate on the paper. Refrigerate until firm.

Gently fold the chocolate "seeds" into the sorbet and freeze until firm.

SAUCES & SPECIAL FAVORITES

These are carefully chosen basic sauces to
go with just about anything you're making.
Isn't it nice to have all the butter sauces in one
place? You'll find my iced tea here because
we couldn't find a good place for it, and guests
love it so we didn't want to leave it out.

236	Mousseline Sauce
	Beurre Blanc
	Homemade Mayonnaise
237	Hollandaise Sauce
	Cumberland Sauce
	Favorite Vinaigrette
238	Homemade Cranberry Relish
	Raspberry Sauce
	Homemade Chutney
239	Caramel Sauce
	Schrafft's Fudge Sauce
240	Deeda's Iced Tea

Matthias Schmutzer. *Jasminum grandiflorum*, c. 1806. Watercolor, opaque painting, and pencil. 13 x 18 ½ in. (33.8 x 46.9 cm).

35

Mousseline Sauce

1 ½ sticks (12 tablespoons) butter
3 egg yolks, at room temperature
1 teaspoon freshly squeezed lemon juice
Ground cayenne pepper to taste
White pepper to taste
¼ teaspoon salt
1 tablespoon hot water
1 cup whipped cream, at room temperature

Note
This can be used on the lobster soufflé
or in place of the Beurre Blanc on
the lobster with vegetables (page 204).
This isn't the traditional method, but it is
easier. The whipped cream makes this light.

Place the butter in a small saucepan and melt over medium heat. Skim off any foam. Combine the egg yolks, lemon juice, cayenne, white pepper, and salt in a blender. With the blender running, drizzle in the hot water in a very thin stream. When the water has been incorporated, drizzle in the melted butter in a thin stream.

Transfer to a bowl and fold in the whipped cream. Serve immediately, or keep warm on top of a double boiler for up to 1 hour.

Makes about 2 cups

Beurre Blanc

1 cup white wine
1 cup white wine vinegar
1 tablespoon minced shallot
1 tablespoon cream (optional)
1 ½ sticks (12 tablespoons)
    unsalted butter, cold and cut
    into tablespoons
¼ teaspoon white pepper

In a small heavy bottomed saucepan, combine the wine, vinegar, and shallot. Bring to a simmer over medium heat, then reduce the heat to low and simmer until the liquid is reduced to a syrup. Be careful not to burn.

Whisk in the cream, if using. Gradually whisk in the butter 1 tablespoon at a time, whisking until incorporated between additions. Season to taste with pepper and strain out the shallots.

Serve immediately, or keep warm on top of a double boiler for up to 1 hour.

Makes about 1 cup

Cumberland Sauce

1 tablespoon arrowroot
¼ cup orange juice
12-ounce jar currant jelly
1 tablespoon thinly julienned orange zest
½ teaspoon dry mustard
¼ cup dry sherry

Note
Wonderful on ham, smoked turkey,
cold chicken, and lamb chops, whether
hot or cold.

Stir the arrowroot into the orange juice. Place the currant jelly in a small saucepan and bring to a boil. Stir in the orange juice mixture, the zest, and the dry mustard. Bring to a boil, stirring constantly, then stir in the sherry.

Makes about 2 cups

Hollandaise Sauce

2 egg yolks
1 tablespoon freshly squeezed lemon juice
White pepper to taste
1 stick (8 tablespoons) unsalted butter,
    at room temperature and cut into
      5 pieces

Put the egg yolks, lemon juice, and white pepper in the top of a double boiler. Leave at room temperature for 30 minutes. Fill the bottom of the double boiler with an inch or so of water and bring to a simmer with the top part still off the heat. When the water begins to simmer, hold the top part of the double boiler over the steam and stir with a wooden spoon. Do not lower the top part into position.

Stirring constantly, add the butter one piece at a time, stirring to incorporate between additions. When all the butter has been incorporated, cook, stirring constantly, until the sauce reaches the thickness of mayonnaise.

Use immediately or keep in a warm place near the stove (but never over hot water or direct heat) for up to 30 minutes.

Makes about ½ cup

Homemade Mayonnaise

1 whole egg, at room temperature
1 tablespoon lemon juice or tarragon vinegar
½ teaspoon dry mustard
Cayenne pepper to taste
½ teaspoon salt
White pepper to taste
1 cup neutral vegetable oil

Note
Frequently we add chopped fresh tarragon
to the mayonnaise. For chicken salad,
we add tarragon and often make it a lighter
mayonnaise by adding whipped cream.
Also, if you want a very classic taste, replace
2 tablespoons of the neutral oil with pure
olive oil.

Place the egg, lemon juice, mustard, cayenne, salt, and pepper in a blender and mix, then process while adding the oil in a thin stream. Keep blending until it reaches the desired consistency.

Makes about 1 cup

Favorite Vinaigrette

Everyone should have a reliable vinaigrette recipe.

2 teaspoons Homemade Mayonnaise
    (recipe above)
1 teaspoon Dijon mustard
½ teaspoon wasabi
1 clove garlic, crushed
1 tablespoon extra-virgin olive oil
1 teaspoon white wine vinegar

Whisk all ingredients together until emulsified. Remove and discard the garlic before using.

Makes about 2 tablespoons

Homemade Cranberry Relish

A classic on turkey or chicken, this is quite fantastic because of the brandy and orange.

14 ounces fresh cranberries
1 small navel orange, unpeeled and
    quartered
1 cup sugar
1 tablespoon brandy
2 tablespoons orange juice

Add the cranberries and orange to a food processor fitted with the metal blade and pulse to chop as roughly or as finely as you like. Add the sugar, brandy, and orange juice and pulse to combine. Refrigerate until serving.

Makes about 4 cups

Homemade Chutney

1 tablespoon extra-virgin olive oil
1 medium Vidalia onion, finely chopped
3 mangoes, peeled, pitted, and diced
2 apples, peeled, cored, and diced
1 cup dried apricots, halved
¼ cup light brown sugar
1 cup honey
¼ cup golden raisins
½ cup dried currants
½ cup dried cranberries
½ cup apple cider vinegar
1 tablespoon Maldon salt
1 ½ teaspoons grated fresh ginger
¼ teaspoon cayenne pepper
¼ teaspoon crushed red pepper
1 orange

Heat the oil in a skillet over medium heat. Add the onion and cook, stirring frequently, until soft and translucent, about 5 minutes. Transfer the onion to a large pot. Add the mangoes, apples, apricots, brown sugar, ½ cup honey, raisins, currants, cranberries, and vinegar to the pot. Stir in the salt, ginger, and both types of pepper.

Cook over medium heat, stirring now and then, until the liquid is reduced to a thick syrup, 1 to 3 hours. (That's a wide range, but the time will vary depending on the water content of the fruits.)

Adjust seasoning to taste. Cool to room temperature. When the chutney is completely cool, zest and juice the orange. In a small bowl combine 3 tablespoons of very finely julienned zest with all of the juice and the remaining ½ cup honey. Stir this mixture into the cooled chutney.

Makes about 6 cups

Note
This is a particularly good chutney that will keep in the refrigerator for one week and also freezes well. Adjust the amount of seasonings to your taste. In summer we add fresh peaches. It is very good on chicken or ham sandwiches as it really peps them up! We use very thinly sliced bread from William Poll for sandwiches to keep them delicate while still being casual and easy.

Raspberry Sauce

Everyone needs a recipe like this in their back pocket. It goes wonderfully with meringues and vanilla ice cream and is sublimely easy.

2 cups (12-ounce package) frozen
  raspberries, thawed
1 tablespoon sugar
Freshly squeezed juice of ½ lemon

Press the thawed frozen raspberries through a sieve to strain out seeds. (Don't skip this step.) Combine the strained raspberries with the sugar and the lemon juice. Whisk together and refrigerate.

Makes about 1 cup

Schrafft's Caramel Sauce

Schrafft's was a New York institution that served old-fashioned food at a lunch counter where young people would go after school and have a sundae.

1 cup packed light brown sugar
½ cup light corn syrup
6 tablespoons unsalted butter
1 pinch salt
½ cup heavy cream
½ teaspoon vanilla extract

In a heavy saucepan, combine the sugar, corn syrup, butter, and salt. Place over medium heat and melt the butter, then bring to a boil, stirring constantly. When it boils, cook for 1 minute, still stirring. Turn off the heat and stir in the cream, then stir in the vanilla.

Serve hot, warm, or cool. To reheat, stir over very low heat. If the sauce separates after standing, whisk it until it's smooth again.

Makes about 1¾ cups

Schrafft's Fudge Sauce

Simply the best fudge sauce.

1 tablespoon unsweetened cocoa powder
1 cup sugar
¾ cup heavy cream
¼ cup light corn syrup
2 tablespoons unsalted butter
2 ounces unsweetened chocolate, chopped
1 teaspoon vanilla extract
1 pinch salt
¼ teaspoon malt vinegar

In a heavy medium saucepan, whisk together the cocoa powder, sugar, and ¼ cup of the cream until smooth. Stir in the corn syrup, butter, chocolate, and the remaining ½ cup cream. Bring to a boil over medium heat without stirring. When the mixture registers 236°F on a candy thermometer, which will take about 3 minutes, remove from the heat and stir in the vanilla, salt, and vinegar. The sauce will thicken as it cools, so you may need to reheat it gently to make it pourable if you don't use it right away.

Makes about 1 cup

Deeda's Iced Tea

This delicious and refreshing iced tea is offered to all guests, even those who are just stopping by for a quick visit.

6 to 7 teabags
1 orange
2 lemons, cut into 12 wedges
8 packets Sweet'N Low
Ice for serving
Fresh mint sprigs for garnish

Note
I use Lipton tea but any type of black tea will do.

Place 4 cups water in a medium saucepan and bring to a boil. Turn off heat and add the teabags. Roll the orange on a cutting board to soften, then halve it and squeeze the juice into the pot, straining out any seeds. Place the squeezed, seeded orange halves in the pot as well. Let the bags steep, pressing them occasionally with a spatula, until the liquid has cooled, then squeeze the teabags into the pot and discard. Transfer the tea to a glass pitcher, leaving the orange in the pitcher.

To serve, squeeze the juice of 2 lemon wedges into a 6½-inch high glass or a pint glass. Add 2 packets of Sweet'N Low to the glass. Fill the glass about one-third of the way with tea and stir to dissolve the sweetener. Fill the glass with ice. Add one lemon wedge and garnish with a sprig of mint.

Serves 4

FAVORITE SOURCES

On the Table

Tablecloths

There is always a tablecloth on the round table in my living room. I use Scotchgard (*scotchgard.com*) on them to prevent major stains and I keep a felt liner on top of the table under the tablecloth. I have a checked silk taffeta undercloth that also stays under many of my tablecloths and peeks out from below their hems. I pay a lot of attention to hem details, often adding a ruffle or a pleated edge. My tablecloths are specially made from fabric from a few favorite houses, and I often customize the colors.

Bennison specializes in hand-printed linen fabrics based on eighteenth- and nineteenth-century English and French textiles, reproduced by the late decorator Geoffrey Bennison. *bennisonfabrics.com*

Chelsea Textiles reproduces antique textiles by hand. *chelseatextiles.com*

Le Manach is a French fabric house founded in the nineteenth-century to produce silk brocatelles, damasks, and lampas that eventually incorporated a large range of cottons in chintz-like fabrics. *pierrefrey.com*

Mitchell Denburg Collection Handwoven textiles and rugs made to order according to traditional techniques at the company's own mill in Guatemala. *mitchelldenburg.com*

Trim

Mokuba, headquartered in Paris, is my favorite maker of trims, ribbons, and passementerie for edging tablecloths and upholstery. Much of their line is available online in the US through East Coast Trimming. *18 Rue Montmartre, Paris, mokuba.fr; 142 West Thirty-Eighth Street, New York, eastcoasttrimming.com*

Napkins

Charvet, the oldest shirtmaker in Paris, makes handkerchiefs in the lightest of cottons, which I have found work beautifully as napkins. Charvet doesn't sell online, but is worth a trip if you're in Paris, as these cloths are a durable luxury and come in what seems like hundreds of wonderful colors. *28 Place Vendôme, Paris, or email at contact@charvet.com or on Instagram @charvet_official*

Flatware

Lo Sabro is a French maker of well-crafted, dishwasher-safe cutlery made of either natural wood shaped like bamboo or actual bamboo. *sabre.fr and available at cutterbrooks.com*

Ceramic Plates and Platters

Bardith is a New York city institution carrying eighteenth- and early nineteenth-century ceramics, including porcelain and faience from England and France. *bardith.com*

Heather Cook Antiques is an Atlanta antique shop with a good selection of vintage Aptware, a type of faience pottery from the town Apt in France, that is marbleized all the way through. I acquired my collection—which is mostly blue and white—years ago from the original makers in Apt. It is not easy to come by anymore, and mostly made to order. *heathercookantiques.com*

La Tuile à Loup is a wonderful shop in Paris that sells hand-made French ceramics and other objects for the home, with an excellent selection of high-quality Aptware. While the shop doesn't have a website, its pieces are displayed on the shop's Instagram and can be ordered by direct messaging or emailing the owner, Eric Goujou. *35 Rue Daubenton, Paris, Instagram @latuilealoup, and email info@latuilealoup.com*

Pearl River Mart offers wonderful, inexpensive blue and white ceramic plates. My favorite plates are from the Sendan Tokusa line. *452 Broadway, New York, pearlriver.com*

Rattan

Amanda Lindroth, an English designer, has a line of well-priced wicker trays with glass inserts and leather handles. *amandalindroth.com*

Cabana is a brand based in Capri that works with artisans to design updates of traditional items. They offer rattan-covered Pyrex cookware, which makes bringing something from the oven to the table attractive, and I always serve iced tea from rattan covered glasses. They also carry woven ceramic cachepots the size of an individual soufflé dish and a white dinner plate edged in bamboo. *cabanagloballuxe.com*

Caspari makes the kind of rattan trays I use at the table or to have individual casual meals with friends in the library. Mine are fitted with plexiglass inserts in the bottom, which I recommend. The rattan trays I most like are rectangular dark brown ones with handles, available from Haven & Co. *havenandcompany.com*

Pottery Barn carries inexpensive, well-designed rattan trays and rattan-covered Pyrex dishes and iced tea glasses. *potterybarn.com*

Flower Arrangements

Ariel Dearie is a wonderful young New York florist inspired by history and botanicals who creates arrangements that have a classic elegance. *www.arieldearieflowers.com*

Mary Krueger is a floral and event designer who will come to your home in New York and do very beautiful flowers for a party. *carmonades@aol.com*

Zezé Flowers has filled my orders for individual flowers, bouquets, and potted plants for many years (and created some of the table flowers in this book). This Upper East Side shop also carries interesting garden-related and botanical antiques. *938 First Avenue, New York, 212-753-7767*

Handcrafted Flowers

Carmen Almon, based in San Miguel de Allende, crafts beautifully hand-painted flowers of all kinds made of tole inspired by old botanical watercolors. *carmenalmon.com*

Clare Potter is a New York ceramic artist who makes single flowers and bouquets from fired unglazed porcelain to which she applies multiple layers of color washes that yield a soft, natural appearance. I have two of her flowers—a white camellia and a pale pink rose—and they float around the apartment and give great pleasure. *clarepotter.com*

Vladimir Kanevsky is a traditionally trained New Jersey-based Russian artisan who makes exquisite cabbage tureens, ravishing leaf plates, and extraordinary flowers and fruit trees of porcelain with tole leaves, ranging in size from small bouquets to large arrangements and topiary trees. *thevladimircollection.com*

In the Kitchen

Emile Henry makes ceramic ovenware from French Burgundy clay, which retains heat. They carry an excellent line of ceramic dishes and ramekins for quiches, tarts, and soufflés, including individual soufflé dishes in a variety of colors. *emilehenryusa.com*

Food52 is an excellent source for recipes and also sells a wide selection of kitchenware. *food52.com*

Nordic Ware, 75-year-old Minnesota manufacturer, makes and offers high quality, commercial-grade aluminum Bundt pans in a variety of shapes. *nordicware.com*

Libeco is my favorite source for dishtowels. This Belgian company makes really wonderful quality linens for the table and the kitchen. I use the Parma and Camaret tea towels in blue. *libecohomestores.com*

In the Larder

Barney Greengrass is a New York deli worth visiting, but if you're not in town it also will FedEx gravlax and Nova Scotia smoked salmon anywhere in the United States. *541 Amsterdam Avenue, New York, barneygreengrass.com, 212-724-4707*

Ideal Cheese has been in New York for more than sixty years and stocks over 250 kinds of cheeses from seventeen countries. It ships nationwide. *942 First Avenue, New York, idealcheese.com, 212-688-7579*

Kelley's Katch sells delicious wild-caught American paddlefish caviar from the Mississippi River Basin in and around Tennessee that can be sent overnight via FedEx packed in ice. *kelleyskatch.com, 888-681-8565*

Solex, started by a former maître d' of Restaurant Daniel in New York, relies on many of the same purveyors that high-end chefs use, including langoustines and lobster from Scotland and fresh truffles from trusted hunters in Europe. *solexfinefoods.com, 212-776-1311*

In the Library

Favorite Books

I am a huge admirer of history and historical biographies—even the fiction and design books I love tend to be historical in some way. I included only two of the many science books I adore here as both are broad and humanistic in their approach. I return to all of these books quite often.

The Greater Perfection: The Story of the Gardens at Les Quatre Vents by Francis H. Cabot
A chronicle of the origins of Cabot's garden in Quebec, and the story of its magnificent expansion by the author over the last twenty-five years.

Civilisation by Kenneth Clark
The book companion to the British art historian, author, museum director, and broadcaster's wildly popular 1960s BBC series of the same name.

Talleyrand by Alfred Duff Cooper
An elegant history of an intellectual statesman, opportunist, and rogue and his enormous contributions to France.

Wellington: The Years of the Sword by Elizabeth Longford
This short biography brilliantly reveals the complex workings of an often misunderstood British military hero.

Pavlovsk: The Life of a Russian Palace by Suzanne Massie
The incredible story of the survivors who carried out the task of restoring the eighteenth-century Russian palace to its original splendor after the siege of Leningrad.

Churchill: Walking with Destiny by Andrew Roberts
The definitive portrait of one of our greatest political leaders.

Paris by John Russell
A lively, intimate, anecdotal history of the city and its inhabitants that was the result of fifty years of wandering its streets, courtyards, and cafes.

Robert Kennedy and His Times by Arthur M. Schlesinger
A chronicle of the short life of the Kennedy family's second presidential hopeful that recounts the forces that shaped him, from his family to his passion for social justice.

The Noonday Demon: An Atlas of Depression by Andrew Solomon
An examination of depression in personal, cultural, and scientific terms that reveals the subtleties, complexities, and agonies of the disease.

The Lives of a Cell: Notes of a Biology Watcher by Lewis Thomas
A humane examination of the complex interdependence of all things. Thomas explores the social aspects of germs, language, music, death, insects, computers, and medicine.

Anna Karenina by Leo Tolstoy
Perhaps the finest novel ever written encompassing love, marriage, sex, faith, imperial Russia, as well as the countryside and city undergoing transition.

Memoirs of Hadrian by Marguerite Yourcenar
A literary reimagining of Emperor Hadrian's difficult boyhood, his triumphs and setbacks, and, as emperor, his reordering of a war-torn world that is as much an exploration of character as a reflection on the meaning of history.

Marie Antoinette: The Portrait of an Average Woman by Stefan Zweig
An intimate portrait of the woman who became queen of France at age fifteen based on her correspondence with her mother and her lover Count Axel von Fersen that takes us from the king's bedroom to the queen's attempted escape, imprisonment, and death at the guillotine.

Favorite Bookshops
Few things are as pleasurable to me as browsing the aisles of a great bookstore.

The Corner Bookstore This neighborhood shop always has a good selection of cookbooks and art books. *1313 Madison Avenue, New York*

Heywood Hill This famous London landmark specializes in building libraries for customers, as well as tailoring monthly book shipments on any topic. *10 Curzon Street, London*

Librairie Galignani The oldest English-language bookstore in Europe opened in 1801; it is my favorite bookstore in Paris for its incredible selection of art books. *224 Rue de Rivoli, Paris*

Rizzoli Bookstore A treasure trove, especially for illustrated books on food, fashion, interior decoration, art, architecture, and design. *1133 Broadway, New York*

The Strand The preeminent New York bookstore, stocking over two million books at any given time. *828 Broadway, New York*

RECIPE INDEX

Illustrated recipes shown in italics.

Beef and Lamb
Beef and Veal
  Edita's Borscht with Brisket, 195
  L'Escalopine de Veau au Champagne, 201
  Louise de Vilmorin's Pot-au-Feu, 201

Lamb
  Gigot de Sept Heures, 200

Beverages
Deeda's Iced Tea, 240

Desserts
Cakes and Tarts
  Blueberry and Blackberry Tart, 224, *115*
  Carrot Cake with Orange Zest, 224
  Deeda's Chocolate Almond Roll, 218
  Pecan Meringue Torte with Raspberries and
    Raspberry Sauce, 219
  Richard Sax's Chocolate Cloud Cake, 216

Chocolate Desserts and Sauces
  Chocolate Leaves, 216
  Deeda's Chocolate Almond Roll, 218
  Jayne's Chocolate Madeleines, 223
  Jayne's Watermelon Sorbet with Chocolate "Seeds," 232
  Richard Sax's Chocolate Cloud Cake, 216
  Runny Crusty Chocolate Soufflé, 218
  Schrafft's Fudge Sauce, 239
  Vesuvius Ice Cream Mold with Chocolate Lace, 231, *158*

Confections
  Almond Meringue, 220
  Chocolate Leaves, 216
  Schrafft's Caramel Sauce, 239

Cookies
  Dora's Lace Cookies, 223
  Jayne's Chocolate Madeleines, 223
  Swedish Spice Cookies, 222
  Thin Oatmeal and Orange Cookies, 222

Fruit Desserts and Sauces
  Anela's Poached Fresh Apple with Walnuts and Honey,
    230, *133*
  Apple Pecan Crisp, 219
  Blueberry and Blackberry Tart, 224, *115*

Compote of Fresh Oranges and Grapes, 230
Jayne's Watermelon Sorbet with Chocolate "Seeds," 232
Fresh Peach Ice Cream with Apricot Sauce, 228
Fresh Pineapple Sherbet, 231
Frozen Lemon Soufflé, 220, *144*
Green Grape Mold with Custard Sauce, 232, *90, 91*
Green Grape Sorbet, 228
Pecan Meringue Torte with Raspberries and
  Raspberry Sauce, 219
Raspberry Sauce, 239
Sorbet à la Banane, 231
Vanilla Ice Cream with Raspberry Puree in Pot de
  Crème Pots, 228

Eggs and Cheese
Cheese
  Chopped Salad, 180
  Gruyère Roulade, 178
  Ina Garten's Spinach and Ricotta Lasagna, 190
  Pasta Soufflé, 185, *101*

Eggs
  Caviar Soufflés, 173, *155*
  Chopped Salad, 180
  Gruyère Roulade, 178
  Lobster Soufflé, 204
  Pasta Soufflé, 185, *101*

Fish, Lobster, and Caviar
Fish
  Dover Sole with Mashed Potatoes and Capers, 206
  Filets de Poisson en Soufflé with Mousseline Sauce, 207

Lobster
  Lobster and Grapefruit Salad, 184
  Lobster Soufflé, 204
  Lobster Tiede Surrounded with Clusters of Vegetables
    with Beurre Blanc, 204, *156*

Caviar
  Caviar Soufflés, 173, *155*
  Homemade Potato Chips with Crème Fraîche and
    Caviar, 174
  Tomato à la Russe, 170, *143*

Fruit
Apples
  Anela's Poached Fresh Apple with Walnuts and Honey,
    230, *133*

Apple Pecan Crisp, 219

Avocados
    Cold Vegetables with Herbs and Vinaigrette, 173
    Chopped Salad, 180
    Coronation Chicken Salad, 182, *105*
    Deeda's Lychee Salad, 172
    Lobster and Grapefruit Salad, 184

Grapes
    Compote of Fresh Oranges and Grapes, 230
    Green Grape Mold with Custard Sauce, 232, *90, 91*
    Green Grape Sorbet, 228
    Moroccan Chicken and Couscous, 184, *115*
    Wild Rice with Grapes and Pecans, 213

Grapefruit
    Harissa-Marinated Chicken with Grapefruit Salad,
        194, *88*
    Lobster and Grapefruit Salad, 184

Lychees
    Deeda's Lychee Salad, 172

Oranges
    Compote of Fresh Oranges and Grapes, 230
    Cumberland Sauce, 236
    Deeda's Lychee Salad, 172
    Roast Chicken with Wild Rice, Orange, and Pistachio
        Stuffing, 198
    Thin Oatmeal and Orange Cookies, 222

Pasta and Rice
Pasta
    Chicken Pasta with Fried Croutons, 191
    Cold Spaghetti Salad, 188
    Deeda's Green Pasta with Vegetables and Bacon, 191
    Fresh Zucchini "Pasta," 188
    Ina Garten's Spinach and Ricotta Lasagna, 190
    Le Cirque's Pasta Primavera, 189
    Pasta Soufflé, 185, *101*
    Truffled Spaghetti, 171

Rice
    Roast Chicken with Wild Rice, Orange, and Pistachio
        Stuffing, 198
    Wild Rice with Grapes and Pecans, 213

Poultry
Coronation Chicken Salad, 182, *105*
Chicken Burgers, 198
Chicken Divan, 199
Chicken Pasta with Fried Croutons, 191
Chopped Salad, 180
Harissa-Marinated Chicken with Grapefruit Salad, 194, *88*
Moroccan Chicken and Couscous, 184, *115*
Pea Salad with Shredded Chicken, 180
Poulet au Gros Sel, 196
Roast Chicken with Wild Rice, Orange, and Pistachio
    Stuffing, 198

Sauces
Béchamel Sauce, 185
Mousseline Sauce, 236
Beurre Blanc, 236
Cumberland Sauce, 236
Hollandaise Sauce, 237
Homemade Mayonnaise, 237
Favorite Vinaigrette, 237
Homemade Cranberry Relish, 238
Homemade Chutney, 238
Raspberry Sauce, 239

Vegetables
Artichokes
    Gruyère Roulade, 178
    Potato and Artichoke Gratin, 213

Asparagus
    Cold Vegetables with Herbs and Vinaigrette, 173
    Lobster Tiede Surrounded with Clusters of Vegetables
        with Beurre Blanc, 204, *156*

Beets
    Chopped Salad, 180
    Deeda's Cold Beet Soup, 167, *115, 116*
    Edita's Borscht with Brisket, 195
    Pea Salad with Shredded Chicken, 180

Broccoli and Cauliflower
    Cold Vegetables with Herbs and Vinaigrette, 173
    Deeda's Green Pasta with Vegetables and Bacon, 191
    Deeda's Iced Cauliflower Soup with Crisp
        Croutons, 164, *129*
    Fresh Zucchini "Pasta," 188
    Jayne's Cauliflower with Puree of Peas, 212
    Le Cirque's Pasta Primavera, 100

Lobster Tiede Surrounded with Clusters of Vegetables
with Beurre Blanc, 204, *156*
Pea Salad with Shredded Chicken, 180

Carrots
Cold Vegetables with Herbs and Vinaigrette, 173
Carrot Puree, 212
Lobster Tiede Surrounded with Clusters of Vegetables
with Beurre Blanc, 204, *156*

Cucumbers
Cold Vegetables with Herbs and Vinaigrette, 173
Lobster Tiede Surrounded with Clusters of Vegetables
with Beurre Blanc, 204, *156*

Haricots Verts
Deeda's Green Pasta with Vegetables and Bacon, 191
Gruyère Roulade, 178
Le Cirque's Pasta Primavera, 189
Lobster Tiede Surrounded with Clusters of Vegetables
with Beurre Blanc, 204, *156*
Poulet au Gros Sel, 196

Lettuce
Chopped Salad, 180
Cold Pea, Potato, and Lettuce Soup, 166
Deeda's Lychee Salad, 172
Gruyère Roulade, 178
Pea Salad with Shredded Chicken, 180

Mushrooms and Truffles
Cold Vegetables with Herbs and Vinaigrette, 173
L'Escalopine de Veau au Champagne, 201
Truffled Spaghetti, 171

Peas
Cold Pea, Potato, and Lettuce Soup, 166
Delicate Vegetable Soup, 166
Fresh Zucchini "Pasta," 188
Jayne's Cauliflower with Puree of Peas, 212
Pea Salad with Shredded Chicken, 180

Potatoes
Cold Pea, Potato, and Lettuce Soup, 166
Crème Aurore, 167
Cold Vegetables with Herbs and Vinaigrette, 173
Delicate Vegetable Soup, 166
Dover Sole with Mashed Potatoes and Capers, 206
Edita's Borscht with Brisket, 195
Fried Potato Ribbons, 210

Homemade Potato Chips with Crème Fraîche and
Caviar, 174
Lobster Tiede Surrounded with Clusters of Vegetables
with Beurre Blanc, 204, *156*
Potato and Artichoke Gratin, 213

Spinach
Ina Garten's Spinach and Ricotta Lasagna, 190

Tomatoes
Cold Spaghetti Salad, 188
Cold Vegetables with Herbs and Vinaigrette, 173
Crème Aurore, 167
Fresh Zucchini "Pasta," 188
Henry McIlhenny's Cold Tomato Soufflé, 181
Le Cirque's Pasta Primavera, 189
Lobster Tiede Surrounded with Clusters of Vegetables
with Beurre Blanc, 204, *156*
Tomato à la Russe, 170, *143*

Zucchini
Deeda's Green Pasta with Vegetables and Bacon, 191
Fresh Zucchini "Pasta," 188
Le Cirque's Pasta Primavera, 189

PHOTO CREDITS

Cover
Ngoc Minh Ngo

Frontmatter
Julia Hetta / Art + Commerce: 2; © Eric Boman: 4.

On Deeda
Helmut Newton, *Vogue* © Condé Nast: 10; © Juergen Teller, All rights reserved: 13; Julia Hetta / Art + Commerce: 14–15; Courtesy of Deeda Blair: 17 (all); Courtesy of Deeda Blair / Rephotographed by Sarah Anne Ward: 18; Ellen Graham: 21; Image and Artwork © 2022 The Andy Warhol Foundation for the Visual Arts, Inc. / Licensed by ARS: 22–23; Courtesy of Deeda Blair / Horst P. Horst: 24.

On Entertaining
Guy DeLort: 30; Ngoc Minh Ngo: 33, 36–37, 40; Horst P. Horst, *Vogue* © Condé Nast: 34, 35; Courtesy of Deeda Blair: 38 (all), 39 top right, 39 center, 39 bottom; Quentin Bacon: 39 top left.

On Inspiration
Courtesy of Deeda Blair / Cecil Beaton: 46; Courtesy of Deeda Blair: 60, 61 (all) 70 (all), 71 (all), 74; Courtesy of Deeda Blair / Rephotographed by Sarah Anne Ward: 72–73 (all); AP Images / Wally Fong: 48; © Jean-Régis Roustan / Roger-Viollet: 49; Pascal Hinous, *Architectural Digest* © Condé Nast: 50; Horst P. Horst, *Vogue* © Condé Nast: 51; Norman Parkinson / Iconic Images: 52; Sarah Sze: 54 top left; © 1998 Kate Rothko Prizel & Christopher Rothko / Artists Rights Society (ARS), New York / Photograph Courtesy of Sotheby's, Inc.: 54 bottom left; © Agnes Martin Foundation, New York / Artists Rights Society (ARS), New York: 55 bottom; Art Collection 3 / Alamy Stock Photo: 56 top; Bequest of Mrs. Charles Wrightsman, 2019: 56 bottom; Purchase, Mr. and Mrs. Charles Wrightsman Gift, in honor of Everett Fahy, 1977: 57; © Eric Boman: 58; Derry Moore, *Architectural Digest* © Condé Nast: 59 left; Gibson Moss / Alamy Stock Photo: 59 right; Ngoc Minh Ngo: 62 top left, 63 top left; REDA & CO srl / Alamy Stock Photo: 62 top right; Richard Champion, *Architectural Digest* © Condé Nast: 62 bottom left; 62 bottom right; Sarah Sze: 63 bottom; Photo by Frank Johnston / The Washington Post via Getty Images: 64; Horst P. Horst, *Vogue* © Condé Nast: 65, 66; Julia Hetta / Art + Commerce: 67; Cecil Beaton, *Vogue* © Condé Nast: 68, 69.

Fantasy Menus
© Nicolas Sapieha / KEA: 78; © The Royal Court, Sweden/ photo Alexis Daflos: 82 (all), 83 (all); José Luis Pérez, *Architectural Digest* © Condé Nast: 84–85; Ngoc Minh Ngo: 87, 88, 90, 91, 101, 102–103, 105, 106, 115, 116, 118, 129, 130–31, 133, 143, 144, 146, 155, 156, 158; Durston Saylor, *Architectural Digest* © Condé Nast: 92, 96 top, 97, 99; Artokoloro / Alamy Stock Photo: 98 left; Courtesy of Deeda Blair: 98 top right; Photo: Christoph Gerigk © Franck Goddio/Hilti Foundation: 110, 111 (all); Courtesy of Deeda Blair: 112–113 (all), 124; © Dylan Thomas: 122–23, 125, 126 top; Pablo Zamora: 126 bottom, 127; Peter Hayden: 134; akg-images: 138 (all), 141; Bridgeman Images: 139 top; Photo by Carma Casula/Getty Images: 139 bottom; The Picture Art Collection / Alamy Stock Photo: 140; akg-images / CDA / Guillot: 150 top; Photo 12 / Alamy Stock Photo: 150 bottom; Marc Deville / akg-images: 151 top; akg-images / De Agostini Picture Library / G. Dagli Orti: 151 bottom; Niday Picture Library / Alamy Stock Photo: 152; Alexey Pavin / Alamy Stock Photo: 153 top; Courtesy of Deeda Blair: 153 bottom.

Recipes
© RMN-Grand Palais / Art Resource, NY: 162, 176; Ngoc Minh Ngo: 165, 171, 175, 179, 183, 197, 205, 211, 217, 221, 225, 229, 233; Bridgeman Images: 168, 186, 214; ÖNB/ Wien, Pk 508/541 (Dahlia): 192; ÖNB/Wien, Pk 508/345 (Clerodendrum): 202; ÖNB/Wien, Pk 508/1129 (Lomelosia): 208; Granger Historical Picture Archive / Alamy Stock Photo: 226; ÖNB/Wien, Pk 508/671 (Jasminum): 234.

Backmatter
Courtesy of Deeda Blair: 250; Julia Hetta / Art + Commerce: 254–255.

William McCormick Blair III

Some years ago, I attended a neuroscience conference at which Thomas R. Insel, MD, then director of the National Institute of Mental Health (NIMH), made an observation that would have a profound impact on me: "We have made great advances at the molecular, cellular, and systems level in our understanding of the brain and its workings. We've got fantastic basic science right. What we haven't yet done is translate that into new treatments or diagnostics for psychiatric diseases. It takes more than drugs."

My years of medical advocacy helped me recognize that a gap persists between our understanding of the biology of psychiatric illness and the practice of psychiatric clinicians. I felt that Dr. Insel's comment was important and needed further examination. My reasons were far from dispassionate; for me, the subject was one with deep personal resonance. In May of 2004, after a long struggle with depression, my son, William, ended his own life. He was 41.

After William's death, I began to concentrate on ways to advance research in the study of the brain. "What is needed?" I asked scientists across the country. "Where are the gaps in our understanding of that realm where laboratory science and the patient work of psychiatric practice intersect, so often without mutual recognition? What are the challenges in communicating across disciplines and in sharing a rapidly growing base of scientific data about the sources of mental illness and its eventual treatment and prevention?"

These questions caused me to reflect, and I realized I could help by funding bold and risk-taking research by the next generation of scientists committed to addressing the causes and treatments of mental illness. With guidance from NIMH, I began framing the outlines of a rigorous peer-reviewed program to connect promising young talents in medical and scientific research with mentors, educators, collaborators and, above all, seed funds to pursue novel and innovative avenues of research in the neurosciences.

Given the magnitude of the problems society confronts in addressing mental illness, it was clear we could not go it alone. Fortunately, having served on the board of the Foundation for the National Institutes of Health (FNIH) for a quarter of a century, I knew where to look for a partner. Thus, it was within the framework of the FNIH and its strong infrastructure that the Deeda Blair Research Initiative for Disorders of the Brain was established in 2016. Through the FNIH's processes and networks, the Initiative has identified and sponsored young investigators who are setting out into what remains largely mysterious terrain. The Initiative provides grants to inspire researchers in their pursuit of a fuller understanding of the human brain in all its mighty scope and fragility. The Initiative is unique in that it provides unrestricted, flexible seed money to creative scientists, giving them the freedom to explore new observations and ideas that may be too scientifically ahead of their time to be funded by traditional research grants. My fervent hope is that the Initiative's work will contribute to the forging of new paths in science with the eventual goal of putting an end to suffering and disability.

In collaboration with the FNIH and NIMH, and guided by the Initiative's own scientific selection committee, the Initiative selected scientists whose work shows exceptional innovation and promise. Launched in 2020, the Initiative's inaugural awards funded three recipients:

Christopher Bartley, MD, PhD, formerly at the University of California San Francisco, now at NIMH, for his research generating patient derived monoclonal antibodies that will serve as the foundational research tools for his immuno-psychiatry research in psychosis.

Sarah Fineberg, MD, PhD, at Yale University, whose work aims to identify and validate early alert markers of relationship rupture in borderline personality disorder (BPD) using digital phenotyping.

David Ross, MD, PhD, is professor and chair of the Department of Psychiatry at the University of Alberta Faculty of Medicine and Dentistry. He spent more than ten years as associate program director for the Yale Adult Psychiatry Residency Program during which time he redesigned the Yale classroom curriculum, including the creation of a longitudinal series of integrative neuroscience courses. Dr. Ross's work at National Neuroscience Curriculum Initiative creates a comprehensive set of open-access resources that will help psychiatrists, other mental health providers, and trainees to integrate cutting-edge neuroscience into every facet of their clinical work. In the past eight years, Dr. Ross and his colleagues have created more than 250 new teaching and learning sessions that have been implemented at more than 200 training programs around the world, a critical first step to addressing the educational gap in basic neuroscience literacy, helping prepare the next generation of leaders in psychiatry.

For further information, or to support this work, go to fnih.org and type "Deeda Blair" into the search bar.

To contact:
Deeda Blair Research Initiative
Foundation for the National Institutes of Health
11400 Rockville Pike, Suite 600
North Bethesda, MD 20852
301-496-9921
deeda.blair.research.initiative@fnih.org

There are many friends and colleagues who have helped with this project, and to each of them, I am deeply grateful.

Andrew Solomon gave so much of his time and thought to the introductory essay despite having much else of greater importance to occupy him, and he was far too generous in his description of me.

My unending gratitude goes to Deborah Needleman for her nonstop talent, ideas, and encouragement.

When I conceived this book and wished to have a special custom fabric made to cover each copy, I reached out to Mitchell Denburg, whose beautiful fabrics and carpets I have long relied on for nearly every surface of my house. He generously offered to create a handwoven cloth to cover the book as a gift to me, but unfortunately, shipping issues relating to the pandemic became an obstacle and we were not able to use it. It is his kindness that means the most to me.

What distinguishes one interesting and beautiful book from another is its visual presentation and the way things come together. For this and for his exquisite typographic sense, I am indebted to Patrick Li, who gave his time and talent to this project as a gift of friendship. In Patrick's studio, Hannah Yassky laid out this rather complicated book so beautifully, and I am grateful for the diligence she brought to the process. I have been fortunate to work with Ngoc Minh Ngo, whose poetic photographs brought my recipes and interiors to a realm beyond my greatest hopes.

At Rizzoli, thank you to publisher Charles Miers for his unwavering support and enthusiasm; Andrea Danese, my editor, was unstoppable in her efforts to make my dreams a reality; Supriya Malik tracked down images torn from magazines or saved from sources now lost to me; Natalie Danford, gave my handwritten recipes the polish of a professional; and Kaija Markoe managed the many production details on this book.

At Condé Nast, I am deeply grateful to Jonathan Newhouse, the chairman of the board, and to Anna Wintour, editor in chief of *Vogue* and global chief content officer for Condé Nast. Both were incredibly generous in allowing me to use old images that appeared over the years in the pages of their magazines. At the Condé Nast archive, I am thankful to Ivan Shaw and Cole Hill.

A number of the flower arrangements in this book were created by my friend of nearly twenty-five years, Cathy B. Graham, an artist, illustrator, and author of *Second Bloom: Cathy Graham's Art of the Table*. I have enjoyed many dinners at her home where her whimsical settings have included flowers hung from the ceiling and the most unexpected objects and figurines placed on the table. Her arrangements with their imaginative combinations are incomparable. Some bouquets were created by Zezé, the florist on whom I have relied since my first day in New York City, as well as by Emily Thompson.

Nothing about this book would have been possible without the remarkable assistance of Rachelle Anterola Verceles who has been keeping everything in my life running in the most cheerful and orderly way for the last sixteen years; it is hard to recount the innumerable ways she has contributed to the making of this book. Suffice it to say that there would likely have been no book without her. Stephanie Marra has expertly managed the complexity of my bookkeeping for more than seventeen years, keeping me sane and solvent and my business letters answered on time.

Bill and I were lucky to have the fantastic Elsa Guayardo cook for us for twenty-seven years. For seven years, we were fortunate to have Christina Rascon, who cooks like a dream and whose soufflés are among the best I've had. Anyone who has been a guest at my home recently has been the beneficiary of Anela Radoncic's thoughtful and gracious manner.

I am enormously indebted to a host of friends who have generously supported the Deeda Blair Research Initiative for Disorders of the Brain since its inception. To Robert G. McKelvey for hours of strategizing and to Cara and John Fry for inspired suggestions, as well as to Margo Blair, the late Buffy Cafritz, Susan Butler Plum, William Crouse, Terence Eagleton, Guy Trebay, Margot and John Ernst, Anne Goldrach, Renvy Grave Pittman, Harold Koda and Alan W. Kornberg, Elizabeth and George Stevens, Michael Meagher and Daniel Romualdez, Steven Meyer, Caroline Milbank, Mary Kathryn Navab, Jamie Nicholls, Elizabeth Peabody, Charles Sanders, Hal Werner, and Ward and Nico Landrigan.

The Deeda Blair Research Initiative for Disorders of the Brain is only able to identify the most deserving and original young scientific minds to support because of the brilliant leaders who serve on its scientific selection committee and advisory board. My everlasting gratitude to Mark Daly, PhD, co-director, Program in Medical and Population Genetics at Broad Institute and founding chief of the Analytic and Translational Genetics Unit at Massachusetts General Hospital; Karl Deisseroth, MD, PhD, DH, Chen Professor of Bioengineering and Psychiatry and Behavioral Sciences, Stanford University;

Ricardo Dolmetsch, PhD, global head of neuroscience, Novartis Institutes for Biomedical Research; Maria C. Freire, PhD, former president and executive director, FNIH; Paul Herrling, PhD, former head of Pharma Research, Novartis Institutes for Biomedical Research, and professor of Drug Discovery Science, University of Basel; Harold Dorris, adjunct professor Neurobiological Institute, Scripps Research Institute; Thomas Insel, MD, former director, NIMH, and president and co-founder, Mindstrong Health; Husseini Manji, MD, global head of neuroscience, Janssen Research & Development, LLC; Samantha Boardman Rosen, MD, clinical instructor in psychiatry, Assistant Attending Psychiatrist, Weill Cornell Medical College; Andrew Solomon, PhD, writer, professor of Clinical Psychology, Columbia University Medical Center; Bruce Stillman, PhD, president, Cold Spring Harbor Laboratory.

Among those who have been my guide in the field of public health, a special thanks to Gregory Curt, former clinical director of the National Cancer Institute and Dr. Max Essex, chair of the Harvard AIDS Initiative, and my most trusted supporter and advisor for forty years.

And to every reader who has bought or received this book as a gift, you too are supporting this work, and I am grateful to you.

Proceeds from the sale of this book will be donated to the Deeda Blair
Research Initiative for Disorders of the Brain.

First published in the United States of America in 2022 by
Rizzoli International Publications, Inc.
300 Park Avenue South
New York, NY 10010
www.rizzoliusa.com

For Rizzoli International Publications, Inc.
Publisher: Charles Miers
Editors: Deborah Needleman, Andrea Danese
Design: Li, Inc., Hannah Yassky, Patrick Li
Production Manager: Kaija Markoe
Rights and Permissions: Supriya Malik
Managing Editor: Lynn Scrabis

Printed in Hong Kong
2022 2023 2024 2025 / 10 9 8 7 6 5 4 3 2 1
ISBN: 978-0-8478-7199-5
Library of Congress Control Number: 2022938273

Visit us online:
Facebook.com/RizzoliNewYork
Twitter @Rizzoli_Books
Instagram.com/RizzoliBooks
Pinterest.com/RizzoliBooks
Youtube.com/user/RizzoliNY
Issuu.com/Rizzoli